Los Angeles Times
STYLEBOOK
A MANUAL FOR WRITERS, EDITORS, JOURNALISTS AND STUDENTS

Los Angeles Times

STYLEBOOK

A MANUAL FOR WRITERS, EDITORS, JOURNALISTS AND STUDENTS

COMPILED BY FREDERICK S. HOLLEY

A MERIDIAN BOOK

NEW AMERICAN LIBRARY

TIMES MIRROR

NEW YORK AND SCARBOROUGH, ONTARIO

NAL BOOKS ARE AVAILABLE AT QUANTITY DISCOUNTS
WHEN USED TO PROMOTE PRODUCTS OR SERVICES. FOR
INFORMATION PLEASE WRITE TO PREMIUM MARKETING DIVISION,
THE NEW AMERICAN LIBRARY, INC., 1633 BROADWAY,
NEW YORK, NEW YORK 10019.

 MERIDIAN TRADEMARK REG. PAT. U.S. OFF. AND FOREIGN COUNTRIES
REGISTERED TRADEMARK—MARCA REGISTRADA
HECHO EN WESTFORD, MASS., U.S.A.

SIGNET, SIGNET CLASSICS, MENTOR, PLUME,
MERIDIAN and NAL BOOKS are published *in the
United States* by The New American Library, Inc.,
1633 Broadway, New York, New York 10019, *in Canada*
by The New American Library of Canada Limited,
81 Mack Avenue, Scarborough, Ontario M1L 1M8

Library of Congress Cataloging in Publication Data

Holley, Frederick S
   Los Angeles times stylebook.

   Bibliography: p.
   1. Journalism—Style manuals.   I. Title.
PN4783.H56   1981   070.4′15   80-28897
ISBN 0-452-00552-3

First Meridian Printing, May, 1981
   3 4 5 6 7 8 9

PRINTED IN THE UNITED STATES OF AMERICA

Preface

No one welcomes this stylebook more than I do. I feel as if an oppressive and feckless old regime is overthrown, and our streets ring with the shouts of liberating troops, fresh and rational.

What the author has wrought here is not a revolution, however, but only a sensible accommodation to the ever-changing front of the language, a dressing of our scattered skirmish lines and a set of rules to be followed in the service of uniformity, clarity, grace, idiom and sense.

Of course new orders are never entirely rational and benign, and before long we may find that peculiar new tyrannies have been imposed on us. In my heart I will never yield, for example, to the rule set forth here for the possessives of singular proper nouns ending in s, though I will of course follow style in the interest of solidarity and the common goal.

I had no hand in the making of this work, aside from a few suggestions that reflected my personal idiosyncrasies, and which, for the most part, were compassionately rejected. I would like it to be noted, however, that my proposal for the restoration of the upper-case initials to *Girl Scout* and *Boy Scout*, which I argued with unrelenting ardor, was finally accepted and incorporated into the canon. I seek no greater memorial.

As the book already has a note on its use, this further appendage has no important function but to praise its author where he may not decently do so himself.

Many of the entries to be found here, so felicitously expressed and illustrated, are the result of tireless research, jesuitical debate and hopeful compromise. Some, in the end, are simply the children of a lonely hubris. But these rare aberrations, and each reader will doubtless find his own, may be taken as a mark of individuality and human frailty in a work that is intelligent, scholarly, aware and sound, and that is written with a humor, economy and grace that a reader seeking style itself should find exemplary.

While the purpose of this book is to improve the quality of our own newspaper, I see no reason for not hoping that it will fall into the hands of others who are entrusted with the care of the language, and improve the quality of life in general.

—JACK SMITH

Introduction

This book is an adapted version of the style manual used by the writers and editors of the Los Angeles Times. Although the title identifies this book as a *"style*book," it also deals with questions of usage, and the difference should be pointed out.

An editor who speaks of "style" is not referring to literary style as exhibited by, for instance, Joan Didion or John Gardner, Saul Bellow or John Updike. Style in this instance concerns the nuts-and-bolts decisions on what to abbreviate and when, what to italicize and what to put in quotes, what to capitalize and under what circumstances, and the like. The editor is also referring to spelling preferences: *glamor* or *glamour, cigaret* or *cigarette, ambience* or *ambiance*. In each of these cases, The Times prefers the latter spelling, but there is nothing intrinsically wrong with the others.

When the same editor talks of "usage," what is being referred to is the way the language is used and the choice of words; this is a matter of grammar, a matter of grace and a matter of idiom. The differences between *biannual* and *biennial*, between *disinterested* and *uninterested* and between *farther* and *further* are matters of usage. Usage is not so idiosyncratic a phenomenon as style, and it relates to the past of the language as well as the present.

The present volume is intended to be of help to anyone engaged in writing or editing—not just Times staff members, not just newspaper people, not just journalism students. It should be noted, though, that the style prescribed in this book is a *newspaper* style, and it differs in some respects from the styles preferred by book publishers and magazine editors.

This stylebook, then, is in some degree a distillation of the standard rules of English and their application to a medium in which speed and clarity are of major importance—a metropolitan daily newspaper. It attempts to establish a greater consistency among the varied styles and usages of the different news services that provide some of The Times' product.

The Los Angeles Times Stylebook faces up to some of the most recent style-and-usage problems that bedevil editors everywhere. Among these are the use of courtesy titles for women, the choice of acceptable terms to be applied to ethnic groups and the use of words or phrases generally regarded as obscene, profane or vulgar. This book treats all three of these issues and provides what it is hoped will be at least temporarily acceptable guidelines in these controversial and sensitive areas.

Please note the "temporarily." Our language is in a constant state of flux, and there can be no permanently definitive decision on the choice between *Latino* and *Hispanic* or between *Asian* and *Oriental*, or on the circumstances under which an obscene phrase may legitimately be used.

To a lesser extent, the same is true of some of the old grammatical problems that have dogged scholars, writers, editors and students for generations. This book endeavors to bring fresh, though hardly radical or innovative, interpretations to bear on the sequence of tenses in indirect quotation, the use of the subjunctive (treated under the entry **were, was**) and the *who-whom* question.

In these cases the book tries to simplify. Its approach to tense sequence is intended to heighten immediacy, and it goes only a little further than does George Curme, whose "English Grammar" is one of the old standbys in the College Outline Series; its approach to the subjunctive is a departure from the traditional but is substantially more moderate than that of some grammarians in its treatment of a grammatical form that the late Theodore Bernstein (of the New York Times, author of numerous books on language and usage) described as "vanishing"; its treatment of *who* and *whom* derives to some extent from Jacques Barzun's "Simple & Direct: A Rhetoric for Writers."

Another area in which The Los Angeles Times Stylebook endeavors to establish guidelines is the use of foreign names. Arabic names, Asian names, Russian names have plagued reporters and editors for decades, but never have they been so ubiquitous as they are today.

The Los Angeles Times receives material from 17 news services, and it is not unusual for them to differ widely in the spelling of an Arabic name. For instance, *Moammar Kadafi* might appear as either *Muammar* or *Moammar* for the first name and variously as *Kadafy, Khadafy, Khadafi, Qadafi, Gaddafi* or *Kadafi* for the last; the stylebook tries to help achieve consistency in the spelling of such names. The usages proposed here for the Russian, the Spanish and the Portuguese are to some extent inspired by the U.S. News & World Report Stylebook for Writers and Editors.

In spite of some adaptations, this book remains very much a Los Angeles product. Many of the examples are drawn from Southern California, and some of the style rules apply primarily to regional peculiarities. But an effort has been made to make such peculiarities applicable to a wider area. For instance, the accepted double redundancy of *the La Brea tar pits* (in which *La* means *the* and *Brea* means *tar*) is a peculiarity from which such forms as *the El Niño current* or *the El Paso newspapers* may be derived.

People of good will and profound scholarship will disagree with some of the entries in this book. And some of these entries may indeed be, as Times columnist Jack Smith put it, "the children of a lonely hubris." Few rules do not have exceptions, and some of those in this book represent an effort at standardization.

The reader may well prefer to regard *data* as a plural noun or *none* as a singular in all instances, but to use *adverse* when *averse* is called for, or to use *presently* when *at present* is meant, is no mere matter of taste. The words mean different things, and should be used according to these precise meanings.

This book was developed to solve certain problems of a certain newspaper in a certain city, and, like any such product, it calls for common-sense applications. Some of the entries derive from research and from interviews with scholars. Some are styles and usages that have become standard with the major wire services and in the newspaper world. All are in some degree the result of my 31 years in the newspaper business, most of them as an editor. Whatever credit is due me, it is credit that should be shared. Let me list a few names:

Arnold Dolin and Ted Johnson of New American Library; George Cotliar, Tony Day and Jack Smith of the Los Angeles

Times; David B. Guralnik, editor in chief of Webster's New World Dictionary of the American Language; Roy H. Copperud, professor and columnist; R. L. Evans, who taught English at Bishops College School, Lennoxville, Quebec; O. W. Riegel, former professor of journalism at Washington and Lee University, and Robert Mason, until recently editor of the Virginian Pilot, Norfolk, Va.

Just one more: my father, the late Rev. Allan John Holley, classicist and clergyman, whose loving and firm inculcation of Latin grammar has made all the difference in the world.

Theodore Bernstein, in the introduction to his last book, said he had noticed a new and slowly developing interest in more careful use of the language. I think he was right, and I devoutly hope that this book is a contribution, however slight, to the living language of Shakespeare, Jane Austen and E. B. White.

FREDERICK S. HOLLEY

August 1980

How to use this book

The Los Angeles Times Stylebook is designed to be used in conjunction with one primary reference source: Webster's New World Dictionary of the American Language, Second College Edition. Exceptions are generally noted as such in the text. Webster's Third New International Dictionary may be used as a backup reference, but the principles and usage of the former should prevail.

It is hoped that most style questions can be resolved with a quick glance at an alphabetical entry. Sometimes, however, an entry may be more discursive and give a substantial number of examples under various subheadings. Such entries are usually indicated by listings in larger boldface, such as **Abbreviations** and **Spanish and Portuguese Names.** Overlapping and cross-references are frequent.

Geographical spellings are based primarily on Webster's New World and then on the National Geographic Atlas of the World. We have not hesitated to make exceptions when they seemed justified.

Los Angeles Times
STYLEBOOK
A MANUAL FOR WRITERS, EDITORS, JOURNALISTS AND STUDENTS

A

a, an Use *a* before consonant sounds: *a historic event, a one-year course, a union, a eulogy.*

Use *an* before vowel sounds: *an honor, an FBI man, an hour, an 1860s costume, an onion.*

A rating, B rating, etc. No hyphen. But: *X-rated, AAA-rated.*

AB, BA Capitalize without periods. Do not separate from name of the holder with a comma: *John Jones BA.* See **Academic Usages.**

Abbreviations and Acronyms

   I. A few words of warning
      A. An unrecognized abbreviation confuses the reader and defeats its own purpose.
      B. Too many abbreviations can leave the reader drowning in alphabet soup.
      C. Very often a general term is preferable to an abbreviation in a later reference.
         First reference: *General Motors* or *General Motors Corp.*
         Second reference: *the corporation* or *the company* or *GM*
         First reference: *National Aeronautics and Space Administration*
         Second reference: *the space agency* or *the agency* or *NASA.*
      D. Do not coin abbreviations or acronyms.
      E. Most institutional abbreviations and acronyms should be spelled out somewhere in the story, usually on first reference.

II. Punctuation of abbreviations

A. All-capital abbreviations do not take periods except when referring to nations, states, cities, persons or the United Nations.

AWOL, BA, CIA, ERA, FBI, GOP, MD, PDT, SOS, USS

D.A., F.D.R., L.A., N.Y., S.D., U.N., U.S.

An exception: *LL.D.*

B. Upper-lowercase abbreviations and lowercase abbreviations generally take periods.

Co., Corp., Calif., Inc., Ph.D., a.m., c.o.d., m.p.h.

C. Abbreviations of technical and scientific measurements do not take periods when used with figures: 2,000 *rpm* (revolutions per minute); 10 *ppm* (parts per million).

Without figures, on first reference or in non-technical contexts: *a silly millimeter longer; calculated in parts per million; thousands of cubic feet (Mcf); 60-millimeter mortar.*

D. Headlines and tabular matter may make freer use of abbreviations to save space or to keep material on a single line.

III. Acronyms

A. The use of acronyms must depend to some extent on how prevalent the entity involved is in the news at a given time:

SALT (strategic arms limitation talks) is permissible while talks are going on or are the subject of controversy but will become less intelligible as the talks become history.

(Note, in this context, that it is permissible to say *SALT talks* in spite of its redundancy. But *SALT* should be spelled out on first reference and varied on later references with *the talks* and *the arms talks.*)

B. Acronyms made up exclusively of first initials are all capitals:

DEW Line (Distant Early Warning Line)
COYOTE (Call Off Your Old Tired Ethics)

C. Acronyms that have become common words in their own right are lowercase:

scuba (self-contained underwater breathing apparatus)
loran (long-range navigation)

D. Acronyms made up of first initials plus other letters are upper-lowercase:

Euratom, Comecon, Caltrans

E. In the case of corporate acronyms, capitalize only the first letter, regardless of the organization's preference:

Amtrak, Exxon, Gemco, Pepsico

IV. Date abbreviations

A. Do not abbreviate:
March, April, May, June, July

B. Abbreviate the other seven months only in specific date usage:
Aug. 25, 1980; August, 1980

C. Do not abbreviate days of the week.

D. Use *AD* before a date, *BC* after it. *5th Century BC* is permissible but not *AD 5th Century*, since *AD* stands for *Anno Domini*, in the year of the Lord, and "in the year of the Lord 5th Century" does not make sense.

Make it: *a.m., p.m., EST, PDT.*

V. Abbreviations in headlines

A. Don't use unnecessary abbreviations.

B. Many all-capital abbreviations are acceptable in headlines:

AFL-CIO, CIA, FBI, FCC, GM, GOP, NAACP.

But not unfamiliar ones: *CEEED* (Californians for an Environment of Excellence, Full Employment and a Strong Economy Through Development).

C. The names of a few cities may be abbreviated in headlines but not in copy: *L.A., N.Y., S.F.* Do not use *Philly* except in direct quotations or for deliberate casual effect.

D. Some otherwise unacceptable abbreviations such as *AF, LAPD, LNG* and *VD* may be used in headlines.

E. The use of *OK, OKs* and *OKd* is acceptable in headlines. In all-capital headlines, make them: *OK'D, OK'S.*

F. All-capital abbreviations present a special problem in all-capital headlines and should be avoided unless they are completely intelligible.

G. Names such as *McNamara* and *MacDonald* also take an apostrophe in all-capital headlines: *M'NAMARA, M'DONALD.*

But never: *MAC'ARTHUR.*

VI. Measurements abbreviations

Abbreviate such terms as *hour, year, mile, pound, meter* and *cent* only in tabular or statistical material. When abbreviated, they all take periods. Note the exceptions in II(C).

VII. Place names

A. Spell out *Los Angeles, New York, San Francisco* and *United States* when used as nouns in copy. *L.A., N.Y., U.S.* and *U.N.* may be used as nouns in headlines and in direct quotations. Otherwise use only as adjectives.

Do not use periods in such terms as *USIA, UNESCO.*

B. Names of U.S. possessions, foreign nations and Canadian provinces should not be abbreviated.

Use *Soviet Union* rather than *U.S.S.R.* or *Russia* to refer to the nation. Use *Soviets* and *Soviet* (noun and adjective) rather than *Russians* and *Russian*, except when referring to the Russian Soviet Socialist Republic. This applies to headlines as well as copy.

But try to say *a Soviet citizen* rather than *a Soviet*.

Russ may be used in headlines only when necessary.

Moscow or the *Kremlin* may be used as a synonym for the Soviet government when there is no likelihood of confusion.

C. Abbreviate the following states in datelines, in legislative identifications, and following the names of communities:

Ala.	Ida.	Mich.	N.H.	S.D.
Ariz.	Ill.	Minn.	N.J.	Tenn.
Ark.	Ind.	Miss.	N.M.	Tex.
Calif.	Kan.	Mo.	N.Y.	Vt.
Colo.	Ky.	Mont.	Okla.	Va.
Conn.	La.	Neb.	Ore.	Wash.
Del.	Md.	Nev.	Pa.	Wis.
Fla.	Mass.	N.C.	R.I.	W.Va.
Ga.	Me.	N.D.	S.C.	Wyo.

See **Datelines.**

D. Do not abbreviate *Alaska, Hawaii, Iowa, Ohio, Utah.*

E. In general do not abbreviate names of cities, counties or such entities as *Long Island* and *District of Columbia*. *Washington, D.C.* may be used in rare instances when necessary for clarity.

F. For address usage, see **Addresses and Street Designations.**

VIII. Names of organizations and institutions

A. Use of abbreviations depends on their general acceptance.

1. A few abbreviations are so common that names need not be spelled out even on first reference: *CIA, FBI, AFL-CIO, GOP, PTA, NAACP,* are acceptable first references, but the full titles should appear at some point in the story.

2. In most cases the name should be spelled out on first reference, and a general term is often preferable on second reference.

3. If an unfamiliar abbreviation is necessary, it should be introduced in parentheses immediately after the spelled-out name.

B. Use *Bros., Co., Corp., Inc., Ltd.* and *S.A.* in full and short-form names. Commas are not used before *Inc., Ltd.* and *S.A.*

Use *Assn.* if the word comes at the end of a name. But spell it out if it occurs earlier.

American Medical Assn., Association of Southeast Asian Nations.

C. *Bureau, department* and *division* should be spelled out in corporate and government usage. But *Dept.* may be used in headlines if used with the name of the department: *State Dept.*

D. While the full name of a government agency is, for instance, *Department of State,* it is acceptable to transpose the elements. But do not transpose when the entity is best known the other way: *Bureau of Standards,* not *Standards Bureau.*

IX. Military ranks before the names of their holders

A. Army

1. Commissioned officers:
Gen., Lt. Gen., Maj. Gen., Brig. Gen. (*Brig.* in British usage), *Col., Lt. Col., Maj., Capt., 1st Lt., 2nd Lt.*

2. Warrant officers: *Chief Warrant Officer, Warrant Officer*

3. Enlisted personnel:
Army Sgt. Maj., Command Sgt. Maj., Staff Sgt. Maj., 1st Sgt., Master Sgt., Platoon Sgt., Sgt. 1st Class, Spec. 7, Staff Sgt., Spec. 6, Sgt., Spec. 5, Cpl., Spec. 4, Pfc., Pvt.

Numerical designations may be omitted if irrelevant.

B. Navy

1. Commissioned officers:
Adm., Vice Adm., Rear Adm., Commodore, Capt., Cmdr., Lt., Lt.(j.g.), Ens.

2. Warrant officers: as above.

3. Enlisted personnel:
Master Chief Petty Officer, Senior First Class Petty Officer, Chief Petty Officer, Petty Officer 1st Class, Petty Officer 2nd Class, Petty Officer 3rd Class, Seaman, Seaman Apprentice, Seaman Recruit

C. Marine Corps

   1. Commissioned officers: same as those in the Army.

   2. Warrant officers: as above.

   3. Enlisted personnel:

     Sgt. Maj., Master Gunnery Sgt., 1st Sgt., Staff Sgt., Sgt., Cpl., Lance Cpl., Pfc., Pvt.

D. Air Force

   1. Commissioned officers: same as those in the Army.

   2. Enlisted personnel:
     Chief Master Sgt., Master Sgt., Tech. Sgt., Staff Sgt., Sgt., Airman 1st Class, Airman

E. Miscellaneous military usages:

   1. Do not repeat rank on second reference except when needed to avoid confusion.

   2. *General of the Army, Fleet Admiral* and *Field Marshal* are to be capitalized and spelled out preceding a name.

   3. Do not abbreviate or capitalize job descriptions or ratings such as *machinist* and *radarman*.

   4. When necessary to refer to a retired officer by rank: *William R. Corson, retired Marine colonel.*

   5. Police departments and fire departments use the same abbreviations as those used by the military. If necessary, use a branch designation before the rank: *Battalion Cmdr., Police Lt., Fire Capt.*

   6. Usages like *LAPD* are to be avoided but are permissible in headlines.

X. Titles

  A. *Gov., Lt. Gov., Sen.* and *Rep.* and their plurals should be used preceding names:
    Gov. Edmund G. Brown Jr.; Mayor Tom Bradley; Govs. Edmund G. Brown Jr. and Hugh L. Carey; Gov.-elect Edmund G. Brown Jr.; former Gov. Ronald Reagan

B. For religious titles see **Religious References.**

C. Do not abbreviate *Postmaster General, Secretary General* or *Treasurer. Supt., Atty. Gen.* and *Dist. Atty.* should be used before a name.

D. Such titles as *assistant attorney general* and *deputy district attorney* should generally be placed after the name of the person, lowercased and set off with commas: *Drew S. Days, assistant attorney general.*

But if it is necessary to use the title in front of a name, make it: *Assistant Atty. Gen. Drew S. Days.*

E. The abbreviations *Atty. Gen.* and *D.A.* may be used in headlines with or without names.

F. Do not abbreviate the title *Deputy* or *Assistant* whether it is a complete title or part of one.

XI. Miscellaneous usages

A. Some abbreviations do not need to be spelled out in any case: *c.o.d., m.p.h., GI, SOS, TB, TNT, TV.*

B. Abbreviate academic and religious degrees and orders as shown: *D.Litt., D.Sc., Ph.D., BA, DDS, MA, DD, SJ.* Do not set off such designations with a comma: *Tracy Jones Ph.D.*

C. Names of colleges and universities may be abbreviated in headlines and on second reference in stories. The unwieldy names of the California colleges and universities may be abbreviated on first reference provided the full name is spelled out later in the story:

UC Davis, SMU, Penn, Penn State, San Diego State, Cal State Fullerton, Cal Poly San Luis Obispo

The Times abbreviates *UCLA, USC* and *Caltech* in all cases.

See **Academic Usages** for a more complete list.

D. *No. 1 draft choice, No. 3 in the polls.*

E. Designation of legislators:
Sen. Alan Cranston (D-Calif.)

Rep. Hamilton Fish Jr. (R-N.Y.)
state Sen. John V. Briggs (R-Fullerton)
Assemblyman Norman S. Waters (D-Lodi)
Rep. Charles H. Wilson (D-Hawthorne)

Name of residence indicated in sworn affidavit of residence is to be used in identifying congressmen from California as well as state senators and assemblymen.

F. Do not abbreviate:
1. Books of the Bible

2. Serial terms (with the exception of *No. 1*, etc.):
Book 2, Chapter 6, Page 17, Section V.

3. Technical jargon from special-interest pages when used in general news pages:

earned run average (not ERA, which is acceptable in sports pages but clearly misleading elsewhere)

special drawing rights (not SDRs, which is acceptable in financial pages)

rhythm and blues (not R&B, which is acceptable in entertainment pages)

G. The preposition *versus* should be used only in referring to court proceedings and sports contests. It should be abbreviated (*vs.*) in each case.

H. Percentages in figures take the percentage symbol except when they occur at the beginning of a sentence.

about   Don't say *at about* in reference to time. *At 10 o'clock* is acceptable, and so is *about 10 o'clock*, but not *at about 10 o'clock*.

The use of *about* is preferable to that of *approximately* or *some* in such a context as: *About 500 people were on hand.*

abrasions, contusions, lacerations   Avoid this long-winded way of saying *scrapes, bruises and cuts.*

absolute   Nothing can be more absolute or less absolute.

Academic Usages

I. Abbreviations

   A. Use the abbreviation *Dr.* on first reference to medical doctors, chiropractors, dentists, optometrists and veterinarians, but make it clear what their specialty is.

   Do not use *Dr.* with holders of the Ph.D. or similar degrees, and do not apply in the case of honorary degrees.

   Do not use *Dr.* (or any other such term) on second reference.

   B. The abbreviation *Prof.* may be used for first reference to those who hold the rank, but *associate professor* and *assistant professor* should be spelled out, lowercase, after the name. The latter should be avoided if possible.

   Prof. Henry Evans; Henry Evans, associate professor

   C. When a person's specialty is included with the title, the phrase becomes an occupational label and should be spelled out, lowercase, preferably after the name:

   Timothy Jordan, professor of history; history professor Timothy Jordan

   Also make it:

   Shirley Jordan, department chairman; department chairman Shirley Jordan

   But if the person holds an endowed chair, make it:

   Shirley Jordan, Walt Whitman Professor of English

   D. The occasion to place degrees after the names of individuals is rare, but the abbreviation is sometimes useful standing alone or in headlines. In either event:

     1. Degrees that are all capitals take no periods:
     AB, BA, DDS, MD, MS

     An exception: *LL.D.*

     2. Abbreviations that are upper-lowercase take periods:
     Ph.D., Ed.D., Th.D.

     3. Do not separate these abbreviations from names with commas: *Timothy Jordan MA, Shirley Jones Ph.D.*

4. When they occur standing alone, it is preferable to refer to them by their generic equivalents:

his master's degree; her doctorate in physics

E. When specialists of various kinds, including medical men, are listed together, the *Dr.* may be used with all of them, but their specialties should be made clear.

II. Capitalize titles with names on first reference:

Dean Charles L. Taylor, Chancellor James K. Walsh

III. Ersatz and misleading degree labels are becoming a problem in the academic world, notably the so-called *ABD* (all but dissertation), which purports to indicate partial progress toward the doctorate. Reporters should be wary of it.

IV. Divisions within colleges and universities that have names of their own or constitute an entity larger than a department should be capitalized:

USC Law Center, Harvard Law School, McGeorge School of Law (at University of the Pacific), *Harvard Graduate School of Business Administration* (or *Harvard Business School*), *UC San Diego School of Medicine, the English department, the physics department.*

It is incumbent upon writers and reporters to get the names of such bodies right and on editors to double-check when doubt exists.

V. Capitalize such usages as:

Rhodes Scholarship
Nieman Fellowship
Fulbright Exchange Scholarship/Fellowship
Woodrow Wilson Fellowship
Sherman Fairchild Distinguished Scholar
Luce Professor of Law and Social Change

VI. Names of colleges and universities should in general be spelled out in full on first reference, and commonly recognized abbreviations may be used in later references and in headlines.

Exceptions: The Times uses *UCLA, USC* and *Caltech* in all references.

Institutions in California's two university systems may be referred to by an abbreviated form on first reference, but the full name should be used somewhere in the story:

UC Berkeley; University of California, Berkeley
UC San Diego; University of California, San Diego
Cal State Fullerton; California State University, Fullerton
Cal Poly Pomona; California State Polytechnic University, Pomona

Note: The University of California, San Francisco Medical Center, may be referred to either as *UC San Francisco* or *San Francisco Medical Center.*

VII. In sport stories, names of colleges and universities may be abbreviated in all references when they are intelligible to the reader.

VIII. Religious titles and usages present a special problem. See **Religious References.**

IX. The California State University and Colleges system uses the following names and abbreviations:

California State College, Bakersfield (Cal State Bakersfield)
California State University, Chico (Cal State Chico)
California State University, Dominguez Hills (Cal State Dominguez Hills)
California State University, Fresno (Cal State Fresno)
California State University, Fullerton (Cal State Fullerton)
California State University, Hayward (Cal State Hayward)
Humboldt State University (Humboldt State)
California State University, Long Beach (Cal State Long Beach)
California State University, Los Angeles (Cal State L.A.)
California State University, Northridge (Cal State Northridge)
California State Polytechnic University, Pomona (Cal Poly Pomona)
California State University, Sacramento (Cal State Sacramento)

California State University, San Bernardino (Cal State San Bernardino)
San Diego State University (San Diego State)
San Francisco State University (San Francisco State)
San Jose State University (San Jose State)
California Polytechnic State University, San Luis Obispo (Cal Poly San Luis Obispo)
Sonoma State College (Sonoma State)
California State College, Stanislaus (Cal State Stanislaus)

accent marks The correct accent marks should be used as appropriate, provided the mechanical department can produce them. In the new Times system, for instance, six such marks will be available: acute, cedilla, circumflex, grave, tilde and umlaut.

accept, except *Accept* means to receive willingly, to agree with. *Except* means excluding, or as a verb, to exclude.
The President accepted a gift from the Dalai Lama.
The President accepted the French proposal.
He took everyone except his daughter, Amy.
He excepted Idi Amin from his congratulations.

accidentally Never *accidently.*

accommodate

according to *Said* is preferable.

acre-foot The amount of water that would cover one acre to a depth of one foot. Note hyphen.

acronyms See **Abbreviations and Acronyms.**

acting Always lowercase before a title: *acting Mayor John Addison.*

acts, amendments, bills, laws Capitalize the name or title of an act, such as *the Taft-Hartley Act* or *the Clayton Antitrust Act,* but not descriptive titles like *the housing act.*
Lowercase descriptions of bills: *fair housing bill.*
Capitalize formal titles of constitutional amendments: *Fifth Amendment, 19th Amendment.*

Do not capitalize informal titles or descriptions of unratified amendments: *women's rights amendment, Prohibition amendment.*

acts of plays *Act II, Scene 1.*

AD It means in the year of the Lord. Use preceding a date: *AD 1979.* Do not say *4th Century AD* or *AD 4th Century.*

BC (before Christ) should follow a date: *202 BC.* It may be used with a century: *4th Century BC.*

Do not use periods with either abbreviation.

Addresses and Street Designations

I. Use only the abbreviations *Ave., St.* and *Blvd.* and these only in street addresses with house numbers or in headlines:

101 Decatur St., 22 Washington Blvd., 260-A Gower Terrace, 88 10th Ave.

II. When street only is being referred to:

1st Street, Decatur Street, Jordan Place, 29th Avenue

III. In referring to more than one street:

Jordan Place and Dexter Boulevard

10th Street and Gower Terrace
26th and Decatur streets (note lowercase usage)

IV. Abbreviate compass points in an address with a house number, but spell out if the number is omitted:
101 W. Decatur St., 26 N. Lakeview Drive
850 J St. N.W.;

L Street Northwest, North Main Street.

Always identify street as avenue, boulevard, circle, terrace or whatever the case may be.

V. An exception to the above: If a street has a letter or a number rather than a name, spell out the compass point:

101 West 1st St., East 2nd St., 202 West 101st St., 2012 West C St.

VI. Highways should be designated thus:
U.S. 101, *Interstate 15, Illinois 34, California 74,*
County 26-A
On second reference, highways may be referred to simply by
state name and number or, for The Times, in the case of
California as *State 74.*

VII. Box numbers thus: *P.O. Box 387, Box 26*

VIII. If the word *Fort* or *Mount* occurs in the name of a com-
munity, spell it out:
Mount Airy, Fort Wayne
But in names of military bases or mountain peaks, use the
abbreviation:
Mt. McKinley, Ft. Lewis

IX. If the word *Saint* appears in a place name, abbreviate it:
St. John's, St. Louis, St. Augustine, St. Lo
An exception: *Saint John, New Brunswick*

X. In general do not use the street addresses of victims of crimes
or other disasters unless these are germane, as when their
homes have been destroyed by fire, mud slide or otherwise.

ad-lib Hyphenate in all cases. Do not italicize.

administration Capitalize all but general usages: *the Kennedy
Administration, the Carter Administration, the Administration,
the Small Business Administration; an administration.*

admit, concede The word *admit* often conveys a connotation of
wrongdoing, and in such cases it is preferable to substitute the
word *concede.*
Connally conceded that he was a Democrat in 1963.
*Kennedy admitted that he acted irresponsibly at Chappaquid-
dick.*

adopt, approve, enact, pass A legislative body *adopts* or *approves*
amendments, ordinances, resolutions and rules; it also *ratifies*
amendments. It *passes* bills and *enacts* laws.

adopted   Use this descriptive adjective only when it is germane.

advance notice   A redundancy. All notice is in advance.

adverbs   The appropriate place for an adverb that modifies a compound verb is in the middle of the verb. Any other position calls for a specific reason.

He has only given money to the cause.

He only has given money to the cause.

He has given only money to the cause.

In these instances, the location of *only* makes a substantial difference to the sense of the sentence.

adverse   See **averse.**

adviser   Not *advisor.*

ae   Generally make this diphthong a simple *e: archeology, orthopedic.*

But there are exceptions: *aesthetic, aegis, Caesarean* and most words in which it is the initial sound.

aegis

aesthetic

affect, effect   *Affect,* as a verb, means to influence: *The scandal will affect the election. Affect,* as a noun, is a technical term that should be avoided if possible.

Effect, as a verb, means to cause: *His election will effect a lot of changes in the system.* As a noun, it means *result: The effect of his election will be devastating.*

Afghan, afghan, afghani   Capitalized, *Afghan* is a noun or adjective referring to the residents of Afghanistan. An *afghan,* lower-case, is a shawl, a carpet or a dog. An *afghani* is an Afghan coin.

AFL-CIO   The abbreviation is acceptable in all cases.

afterward   Not *afterwards.*

age   Always use figures to denote age, whether of a person, an animal, a book or a movement. But note that duration is not the same thing as age, and spell out numbers denoting it:

He wound up a six-week tour of the world.

The phrase *years old* is unnecessary when the context makes it clear. The same applies to *age 22* or *aged 22*.

The age of a person should be used only when it is relevant.

agenda Takes a singular verb: *The agenda is long and complicated.*

agree to, agree with *Agree to* means to give assent to: *The President agreed to the British proposal.*

Agree with means to be in accord with: *The President agreed with the prime minister.*

Agreement of Subject and Verb

There is a story about an idiosyncratic editor who insisted that the word *news* was plural and that it should take plural verbs and pronouns. One day he wired one of his correspondents:

"*Are there any news today?*"

The correspondent wired back:

"*Not a new.*"

The British say, "The government are . . ."
The Americans say, "The government is . . ."
The British also consider many other words denoting groups of people, such as *company* and *board*, to be plural.

I. These items serve to dramatize the confusion that sometimes sets in when we are dealing with agreement of subjects and predicates. Few of us have much trouble with such specific collectives as *class, committee, crowd, family, group, herd, orchestra* and *team*, all of which usually take singular verbs and singular pronouns. But when we come to such words as *number, total, couple, data* or *none*, some of us tend to come unglued.

Even with the simpler collectives, there are times when the sense demands a recasting of the sentence:

The jury was sent back to its deliberations.

But:

The members of the jury were sent to their bedrooms for the night.

II. Subjects taking singular verbs:

data

> Historically the plural of the Latin *datum*, this word has come to be generally felt as singular and should take a singular verb:
>
> *The data is extremely convincing.*

agenda

> The same principle applies:
>
> *The agenda is long and complicated.*

news

> Historically the plural of the Middle Latin *novum*, this word is invariably singular today:
>
> *Is there any news today?*
>
> *The news from Africa is depressing.*

either, neither, each

> These pronouns take singular verbs:
>
> *Either is correct.*
> *Neither version is correct.*
> *Each of us is going to receive a check.*
> *All of us are going to receive checks.*
> *Neither of the two candidates was acceptable.*

no one, nobody, everyone, everybody, anyone, anybody, someone, somebody

> Indefinite antecedents of this kind almost always take a singular verb:
>
> *No one (or nobody) knows the secret.*
> *Somebody surely has the answers.*
> *Everybody is expected before 9 a.m.*

III. *Personnel, clergy* and *police* are plural, both in sense and in agreement:

> *The police have surrounded the house.*
> *The clergy are divided on the issue of abortion.*
> *Naval personnel were ordered to report immediately.*

IV. Singular or plural:

number, total, variety

There is a simple and generally accepted rule that covers the agreement of these words: If one of them is preceded by *the*, it should be regarded as singular; if it is preceded by *a* it should be regarded as plural:

The number of veterans applying for benefits is smaller than it was last year.

A large number of veterans have applied for benefits.

The total of eligible veterans seems to diminish each year.

A variety of courses have been designed for minority groups.

couple

When used in the sense of two persons, the word takes plural verbs and plural pronouns:

The couple were married Monday. They will return from their honeymoon Saturday.

But when *couple* is used in the sense of a single unit, it takes a singular verb:

Each couple was asked to contribute $10.

handful, lot

Each of these collectives may also be either singular or plural:

A lot of trouble was caused by the lack of cooperation.

A lot of people were killed in the earthquake.

A handful of change was lying on the table.

A handful of men were standing on the street.

majority

When *majority* means *most of*, as it frequently does, it should be handled thus:

The majority of the union was in favor of the strike.

The majority of students were in favor of the sit-in.

Here the number of the verb depends on what professional grammarians call "attraction"—the number is determined not by the word itself, but rather by the noun following it, to which it is "attracted." In the first instance, the word is singular because *union* is singular; in the second it is plural because *students* is plural.

percent

The rule of attraction prevails here, too:

Ten percent of the faculty is in favor of having a student on the board of trustees, and 90% of the students support the proposal.

Here the verb is attracted in the first instance to *faculty* and in the second to *students*.

none

Here, too, the principle of attraction prevails:

None of this nonsense is significant.
None of these apples are ripe.
None of the committee was absent.
None of the students were absent.
None but the brave deserve the fair.

people

Sometimes a collective noun, *people* also is sometimes the plural of *person*:

The people is a great beast. (collective noun)
Six people were killed in the freeway collision. (plural of person)

politics, ethics, economics, etc.

Words ending in *-ics* are singular or plural depending on the sense in which they are used:

Politics is my job; his politics are conservative.
His ethics are deplorable.
Economics is a dismal science.
The mathematics of the plan make it impossible.

some, more, all, any, half, rest, remainder, most, a lot

These words may take singular or plural verbs depending on the sense:

Some of the money is missing.
All of the men are going.

Is any of the money still there?
Are any of the men going?
Half of the money is missing.
Half of the men are coming back.
The rest of the money is still there.
Most of the men are still here.

neither, nor; either, or

When subjects of different number or different person are connected by *nor* or *or*, the verb agrees with the nearest subject:

Neither the reporters nor the editor was responsible.
Neither the editor nor the reporters were responsible.
Neither you nor I am responsible.

V. Rock groups and athletic teams:

Some of these groups have singular titles when a plural might be expected. When such titles are singular, they should take singular verbs and singular pronouns.

The California Surf is . . .
Led Zeppelin was . . .
The Salt Lake City Jazz wins . . .
The Knack plays its . . .

agribusiness

air bag   Two words.

air base   Two words. U.S. air bases in the United States are described thus: *Vandenberg Air Force Base*. U.S. bases abroad use: *Clark Air Base*. The abbreviation *AFB* is acceptable in headlines only and should be avoided then if possible.

air conditioning   Hyphenate the adjective but not the noun:
His business is *air conditioning*.
He is in the *air-conditioning* business.

aircraft names   A few examples of Times usage:
Air Force One, Spirit of St. Louis, Boeing 707, A-4 Skyhawk, F-86 Sabre, F-100 Super Sabre;

DC-10, C-5A, MIG-21, TU-144;
DC-8s, C-5A's, 747Bs;
Apollo 10, Soyuz 228.

air force Capitalize *U.S. Air Force, the Air Force, Air Force unit.* Lowercase forces of other countries unless the formal appellation is used: *British air force, Royal Air Force.*

Air Line Pilots Assn. Note the two-word usage of *Air Line.*

airlines, airways Always check the name of any carrier to determine the correct usage. The World Aviation Directory is a good source. A few examples:

Airlines: Alitalia, Allegheny, American, Continental, Eastern, Frontier, National, Northwest, Republic, Trans World, United, Western

Air lines: Delta, Japan, Ozark, Korean

Airways: Braniff, British, Pan American World, Qantas, South African, World

Other usages: Aer Lingus, Aeromexico, Air California, Air Canada, Air France, Air-India, Swissair

airports Capitalize the word *airport* when it is part of a proper name. The proper names of airports vary widely and should be checked in the World Aviation Directory.

When the name of an airport is truncated, the word *airport* should be lowercased. An exception: The names of people may be cut to the last name without such lowercasing. For instance:

Los Angeles International Airport, Los Angeles airport
Burbank-Glendale-Pasadena Airport, Burbank airport

John F. Kennedy International Airport, Kennedy International, Kennedy Airport
John Wayne Airport, Wayne Airport

airtight One word.

airwaves One word.

al, el See **the** and **Arabic Names.**

à la Not *àla.* Note grave accent.

Alabamian Noun and adjective. Not *Alabaman.*

Alaska Do not abbreviate.

all- Hyphenate all adjective combinations: *all-out, all-around, all-state*. In capitalized combinations: *All-American* in every instance.

Do not hyphenate adverbs: *He went all out; it was all gone.*

allege Use carefully. The source of any allegation must be specified. In criminal cases the sources must be official.

Avoid redundancy. It is correct to say: *Police alleged that Smith killed his wife*. But not: *Police accused him of allegedly killing his wife*.

Do not use *alleged* as a routine qualifier.

Bear in mind that the use of *alleged* does not protect against a libel suit.

Allies Capitalize when referring to the combination of the United States and its allies in both world wars. Also capitalize *Axis* when referring to the Rome-Berlin-Tokyo Axis of World War II.

all right Two words. Not *alright*.

allude, refer To *allude* to something is to refer to it without mentioning it by name. To *refer* to it is to mention it by name. The same is true of *allusion* and *reference*.

She alluded to her former husband, saying, "There is at least one person who disagrees with my position."

She referred to her former husband, saying, "I am sorry that Walter disagrees with my position."

allusion, illusion, delusion An *allusion* is an indirect reference; an *illusion* is a false perception; a *delusion* is a false belief.

also-ran Hyphenate the noun.

altar, alter An *altar* is a religious structure. To *alter* is to change.

alternate, alternative *Alternate* means occurring by turns or to take turns doing something. An *alternate* is a person who substitutes. *Alternative* means providing a choice, one of the things to be chosen or the choice itself.

Use *alternate* or *alternately* to express the sense of one after the other: *We intend to alternate our duties, working on alternate days.*

Use *alternative* or *alternatively* to express the sense of one or the other: *We found that there was no alternative to full-time work every day.*

altiplano   Lowercase and italicize.

alumnus   The Latin forms persist: *alumnus, alumna, alumni, alumnae.*

ambassador-at-large   Capitalize before a name: *Ambassador-at-Large W. Averell Harriman.*

ambiance   Not *ambience.*

A.M.E. Zion Church   Not *A.M.E.Z. Church.* See **Religious References.**

amendments   Capitalize only the official titles of constitutional amendments and only after their ratification: *the First Amendment, the 18th Amendment, the Prohibition amendment, the equal rights amendment.*

Use numerals to denote all amendments above the Ninth.

American Legion, the legion, a legionnaire

amid   Not *amidst.*

amok   Not *amuk* or *amuck.*

ampersand   Use in abbreviations and full proper names of companies and corporations: *AT&T, C&O; Procter & Gamble, International Telephone & Telegraph (but ITT), U.S. News & World Report, Atchison, Topeka & Santa Fe.*

Do not use in names of government bodies.

Limit such usages as *R&B* and *R&R* to the entertainment pages.

"angel dust"   A slang term for phencyclidine (PCP). Put in quotation marks.

Angelenos   Residents of Los Angeles.

Angkor The temple complex in Cambodia is *Angkor*. *Angkor Wat* is an individual temple in that complex.

Anglo- Always capitalize. No hyphen when the second part of the word is lowercase: *Anglophile, Anglophobe*.

Use hyphen when the second part is capitalized: *Anglo-American*.

As a noun or adjective standing alone, *Anglo* should be used in stories in which *Anglo* is opposed to *Chicano*. In other contexts, *white* is the preferred term. See also **Ethnic Designations**.

Anglo-Catholic Certain members of the Anglican and Episcopal churches. See also **Religious References**.

angry One is angry *about* an occasion, a situation or a condition. One is angry *with* people, and one is angry *at* things or animals.

animals Personal pronouns should not be used in referring to an animal unless its sex has been established or it has a proper name:

The rabbit was frightened; it fled.
Lassie was frightened; she barked.
The ram lowered his head.
The mare flicked her tail.

Capitalize names of animals, and use Roman numerals to show descent: *Whirlaway II*.

For breed names, follow Webster's New World Dictionary. If the breed is not listed, capitalize names derived from proper names.

If a zoological name is used, capitalize the genus (but not the species) and italicize the entire phrase: *Homo sapiens*. Second reference: *H. sapiens*.

annual An event cannot be called *annual* until it has been held for consecutive years. It is proper to say that it is intended to be held annually.

antennae, antennas Use *antennae* when speaking of the organs of insects or figuratively to refer to a person's awareness or sensitivity. Use *antennas* for TV attachments and similar devices.

anti- To be consistent with the style of the wire services, hyphenate all except the following, which have meanings of their own: *antibiotic, anticlimax, antibody, antidepressant, antidote, antifreeze, antigen, antihistamine, antimatter, antimony, antiparticle* (and similar scientific terms), *antipasto, antipathy, antiperspirant, antiphon, antithesis, antitrust*
Some of the hyphenated usages: *anti-aircraft, anti-bias, anti-poverty, anti-Semitic, anti-war.*

anticipate, expect To *anticipate* means to expect and prepare for something. To *expect* does not include the idea of preparation: *They expect a record crowd; they have anticipated it by setting up more bleachers.*

any- *Anybody, anyhow, anymore* (as an adverb), *anyone, anyplace, anyway, anything, anytime.* Never *anyways.*

any more Two words as an adjective: *We don't have any more bananas.* Note, too, that both the adjective and the adverb should generally be used in a negative context.
Sally doesn't live here anymore.
There isn't any more work.

apostle Lowercase except when used with proper name: *St. Paul the Apostle.*

apostolic delegate, papal nuncio An *apostolic delegate* is a papal envoy to a nation that does not have diplomatic relations with the Vatican. A *papal nuncio* is an envoy to a nation that does have such relations.

apostrophe See **Punctuation.**

apparent An overused qualifier. To say *He died of an apparent heart attack* is wrong. Apparent heart attacks don't kill. Make it *He died, apparently of a heart attack* or *He died of what appeared to be a heart attack.*

approve See **adopt.**

approximately A verbose way of saying *about.* Avoid it.

April Fools' Day Note apostrophe.

Arabian Peninsula

Arabic Names

I. Arabic names present a continuing problem because the spellings often vary with whether the transliteration was done by an Englishman or a Frenchman; because usages vary from nation to nation, and because some nations historically have a multiplicity of acceptable spellings. Some frequent difficulties are addressed here:

II. *El* and *al* (both meaning *the*)

    A. Both should be eliminated from the names of persons except in direct quotations and in formal references to royalty, such as the Emir of Kuwait:

        Anwar Sadat, Sheik Jabbar al Ahmed al Sabah

    B. When the use of *al* or *el* is necessary, it should be lowercased without a hyphen when the complete name is used but capitalized without a forename on second reference.

    C. In the case of royalty or direct quotations, use *al* when the nation involved has been English-influenced, *el* when it has been French-influenced:

        el in Lebanon, Syria, Algeria, Morocco, Libya, Tunisia, Egypt

        al in Saudi Arabia, United Arab Emirates, Jordan, Iraq, Bahrain, Kuwait, Oman, Qatar, Yemen, South Yemen

    D. Retain the *el* and the *al* in place names:

        Al Karak, El Arish, El Alamein, Sharm el Sheik, Ras al Geneina, Algeciras, Algiers, Alhambra

III. *Abdul* and *Abdel*; *Abdulaziz* and *Abdelaziz*

One word in all cases. Use *Abdul* in Iran, Jordan and the Arabian Peninsula, *Abdel* in Lebanon, Syria and North Africa.

Note that *Abdul* is generally used as a compound surname. Abdul-Jabbar is on safe ground in using both elements as his surname.

IV. *Ibn, bin* and *ben* (meaning *son of*)

    A. They are different transliterations of the same word.

    B. *Ibn* is preferred in Arab countries east of and including Egypt.

C. *Ben* is the preferred usage in North Africa, except for Egypt.

D. *Bin* should be replaced by the appropriate one of the other two.

(There is a place for *bin*, however: in Southeast Asia, where it is the generally preferred form. See **Asian Names.**)

E. *Ibn* and *ben* should be lowercased with full names but uppercased on second reference:
Ahmed ben Bella, Ben Bella

V. *Abu* is a prefix similar to *ibn* but meaning *father of*. It should be used as *ibn* and *ben* are.

It is worth noting that *Abu* is used as part of an alias by many members of Palestinian underground groups. In general, such aliases should be used.

VI. *Khadafi, Kadafy, Qadafi, Kadafi*

A. These varying transliterations of the name of the Libyan leader sum up many of The Times' problems with Arabic. They represent different, though similar, pronunciations.

B. For The Times' purposes, let us make it *Kadafi*, and let us apply the same principle to other Arab names:

a *k* rather than a *kh* or a *q*
an *i* rather than a *y*

(Note that this is in contrast to a similar usage in Persian, the language of Iran, where the letters *gh* are to be preferred to the *q*.)

C. An exception: the nation of Qatar, since it is commonly so spelled, and other generally recognized place names.

VII. First names: *Hussein, Ahmed, Faisal, Hakim, Karim, Adib, Said.*

VIII. In spite of the phonetics, spell it *sheik*. Note the feminine *sheika*.

IX. *Mohammed, Muhammad,* etc.

A. Prominent Arabs have adopted their own preference, and The Times should try to ascertain that preference and abide by it.

B. When no preference is available or when sources are in conflict, use standard American usage: *Mohammed.*

X. Second references

A. Some Arabic names use the first element on second reference, others the second:

Kaboos ibn Said, Kaboos
Anwar Sadat, Sadat

B. Why? Because Kaboos is a member of royalty and Sadat is not.

XI. *Moslem, Muslim*

Most of Islam's faithful prefer *Muslim,* and Arabists say it is more correct. Make it *Muslim* in all contexts.

arbitrate, mediate An *arbitrator* gives a binding decision in a dispute. A *mediator* may make a suggestion and tries to persuade the parties to agree.

arch- In general do not hyphenate:
archdeacon, archbishop, archenemy, archvillain, archrival, archduke. But: *arch-Republican.*

Use *arch* as an independent adjective only in its meaning of clever, crafty, mischievous or pert: *an arch look.*

Archbishop of Canterbury But lowercase other archbishops except *Archbishop of York.*

archdiocese Capitalize when used with a proper name: *the Archdiocese of Los Angeles.*

The same applies to *diocese: The Diocese of Brooklyn.*

archeology

Arctic Capitalize except when used casually to mean very cold.

area codes (123) 456-7890.

army Capitalize when referring to U.S. armed forces: *U.S. Army, the Army, Army barracks.*
Lowercase forces of other nations: *British army, Soviet army.*
But capitalize formal or informal appellations when known: *the British 8th Army, Red Army, People's Liberation Army.*

arrange It is redundant to say *arrange in advance.*

Art Deco

Arts and Letters

I. Newspaper style differs considerably from the style of book and many magazine publishers. Italics—which are used in this book to indicate examples of the point being made, *not* to indicate that a word or phrase should actually be in italics—are avoided except as explained below and under **Italics.**

II. Books and written materials

A. Capitalize the titles of books, including both prepositions and conjunctions of four letters or more:
"*Fear of Flying,*" "*The Rise and Fall of the Third Reich,*" "*Gone With the Wind,*" "*Of Mice and Men*"

B. Put quotation marks around the names of all such titles, as shown above, except the Bible, the Koran, similar sacred books and generally accepted reference volumes:
Jane's Fighting Ships, Encyclopaedia Britannica (note spelling), *Webster's New World Dictionary of the American Language, the World Almanac, Who's Who, Columbia-Lippincott Gazetteer of the World, Lloyd's Register of Shipping, Congressional Quarterly*

But do use quotation marks around works of a scholarly or reference nature that are largely the work of individual authors:
Bergen Evans' "A Dictionary of Contemporary English Usage," George O. Curme's "English Grammar"

C. Capitalize, but do not use quotation marks around, the names of magazines and newspapers; do not capitalize the initial article:

the Los Angeles Times, the New York Times, the Reader's Digest, the Nation, Harper's Magazine, Time magazine, the New Yorker, New West, New York magazine, the New Republic, the Atlantic Monthly, the Wall Street Journal, U.S. News & World Report

In titles of foreign publications, the initial article should be retained:

Al Ahram, Die Welt, El Pais, Il Giorno, La Prensa, Le Figaro

D. Capitalize and use quotation marks with titles of poems, short stories, essays and similar short compositions:

"The Snows of Kilimanjaro," "Stopping by Woods on a Snowy Evening," The Superannuated Man," "The White Negro"

E. The titles of newspaper stories are their headlines, and these should likewise be capitalized with quotation marks:

"Senate Ratifies 2nd Pact, Yielding Canal to Panama"

III. Music

A. Generic titles should be capitalized without quotation marks:

Symphony No. 4 in D Minor, Beethoven's Fifth Symphony (Either form of the number is acceptable.)
Concerto in E Minor for Violin, Sinfonia Concertante in E-flat for violin and viola

Note use of hyphen and varying capitalization depending on whether identification of key or instruments is part of the title. Titles should be looked up in Schwann Record and Tape Guide, any issue.

B. Descriptive (one-of-a-kind) titles and nicknames require quotation marks:

"Rhapsody in Blue," "The Bartered Bride," "Symphonie Fantastique," the *"Eroica"* Symphony, the *"Unfinished"* Symphony

(These, too, may be checked in the Schwann guide.)

C. Names of operas, arias and songs, classical or popular, should always go in quotation marks, along with names of records, and albums unless they are generic as in III(A) above. Song titles should be upper-lowercase, in accordance with U.S. usage.

D. Names of characters in operas (and plays) do not take quotation marks.

E. Foreign musical terms need no special attention if they have become common usage in English. They should not be in italics; do not be misled by the style of this book, which is to use italics for examples. The following, and similar familiar terms, should not be in italics:

aria, adagio, pas de deux, pianissimo

Less familiar terms, but not titles, should be set in italics.

F. The language of a musical title depends on the language in which it is performed at a given time.

Performed in French, the cantata by Debussy should be referred to as "L'Enfant Prodigue"; sung in English, it is "The Prodigal Child."

Compositions that are instrumental only or are being referred to apart from a specific performance should be rendered in their best-known titular form.

G. One person, or one person plus an accompanist, gives a *recital*; two or more people give a *concert*.

H. Use the generally accepted American spellings of Russian names in the musical world. For instance:

Tchaikovsky, Mussorgsky, Glazunov, Prokofiev, Rachmaninoff

I. Such popular music terms as *R&B* and *R&R* are acceptable only in music features, columns and reviews. Elsewhere, make it: *rhythm and blues, rock 'n' roll*

IV. Painting, sculpture and architecture

A. All titles should be capitalized and placed in quotation marks:

"Mona Lisa," "Guernica," "The Thinker," "David," "Venus de Milo"

B. Capitalize artistic styles and movements but lowercase general usages:

Art Deco, Bauhaus, Beaux-Arts, Dada, Gothic, Impressionist, Op Art, Romanesque

But:

classical (following Greek or Roman style)
baroque (fantastically ornate)
gothic (eerie, forbidding)
modern (spare, geometric)

For instance: *a Gothic cathedral, a Gothic novel, a gothic atmosphere*

V. Films, radio, television and theater

A. Capitalize, and place in quotation marks, all names of films, radio and television plays and stage productions:

"The ABC Evening News," "The Ox-Bow Incident," "The Harvey Girls," "The Harvey Korman Show," "Laverne and Shirley," "Roots," "MASH," "Lou Grant," "The Hanna-Barbera Happy Hour," "Hello, Dolly!" (note punctuation)

Dropping of quotation marks and use of abbreviated forms is acceptable in TV schedules, but uniformity of usage is the goal.

B. In stories dealing with events or programs that have a sponsor's name as part of their titles, such as "Hallmark Hall of Fame" or MONY (Mutual of New York) Tournament of Champions, the name of the sponsor should be used only once, preferably on first reference, in a story. It should be avoided in headlines.

C. Capitalize the first letter of *radio* when used before a name to indicate an official voice of the government: *Radio Moscow.*

Lowercase and place after a name to indicate merely that information was received from broadcasts in a city: *Havana radio.*

A usage such as *Radio Free Europe* is a proper name.

D. Lowercase *radio station* and *television station* when used before call letters: *radio station KHJ, television station KABC.*

E. Also capitalize and spell out: *Channel 2*. But *Ch. 2* is permissible in tabular material and in schedules.

F. Use *television* and *TV* as desired in reference to the medium, but avoid *video* except in proper names and such generally accepted compounds as *videotape*.

G. The phrase *prime time*, as used in contrast to daytime television, should be two words, in accordance with the dictionary. Hyphenate the adjective.

H. The names of television networks may be abbreviated in leads and elsewhere in stories but the full name must be spelled out at some point.

Note that *CBS Inc.* is the official name of the parent company and that *ABC* stands for American Broadcasting Cos. (plural).

I. The word *theater* should be spelled with an *-er* ending in all generic usages. In titles the usage of the particular theater involved should be followed. When the usage is not known, the *-er* ending should be used, but an effort should be made to ascertain the preference.

artwork   One word.

Asian Names

This section is the result of interviews and correspondence with a number of Asian authorities. Some liberties have been taken with their suggestions in the interest of coherence and simplicity.

It should be borne in mind that, as with other foreign names, the personal preferences of Asians in public life are to be honored, even when they diverge from our standards.

BANGLADESH AND PAKISTAN

A. The people of these countries are Bangladeshis and Pakistanis. The appropriate adjectives are *Bangladeshi* and *Pakistani*, but the language of Bangladesh is *Bengali*.

B. *Zia ul-Haq* and *Ziaur Rahman:* These are generally accepted spellings of the names and should be followed. In each case, *Zia* is an acceptable second reference, but full names should be used when necessary to avoid confusion.

C. In other instances, omit the *ul* and the *al* from Bangladeshi and Pakistani names.

D. Use the last element of all other Bangladeshi and Pakistani names on second reference, except those ending with *Khan.*

E. When a name ends with *Khan,* use it along with the preceding name on second reference: *Yahya Khan, Habibullah Khan.* Note that these are names, not titles.

Some names begin with the title *Khan* and end with the name *Khan: Khan Abdul Gaffar Khan.* Such titles should be used on first reference except when another title is used. Thus:

Khan Abdul Gaffar Khan (first reference)
Chairman Abdul Gaffar Khan (first reference)
Dr. Abdul Gaffar Khan (first reference)
Gaffar Khan (second reference)

BURMA

A. Burmese names generally consist of two one-syllable words. In such cases use the full name on second reference as well as first. When the name consists of more than three words, use the last two on second reference.

B. The greatest problem with Burmese names is the use of honorifics, among them: for women, *Daw* (for older women), and *Maa* (for younger women); for men, *Naw, Saw, U* and *Maung.*

C. Such honorifics may be appropriately used on first reference, except when another title is used: *U Ne Win* or *President Ne Win.*

D. On second reference, drop all honorifics except when The Times would use the feminine honorifics in accordance with its policy on courtesy titles.

E. *Maung* and *U* may be either honorifics or name elements. In the case of *Maung U Shan Maung,* for instance, the first *Maung* is a title and the *U* and the second *Maung* are name elements. The appropriate second reference: *Shan Maung.*

CAMBODIA

A. Most names are brief, and it seems appropriate generally to use both elements on second reference: *ousted Premier Pol Pot, Pol Pot.*

B. An exception: *Norodom Sihanouk,* to whom we should refer on second reference as *Sihanouk.*

CHINA

A. The Times uses the Pinyin method of romanizing names for almost all people and places in the People's Republic of China.

    1. There are a few place-name exceptions: *Canton, Inner Mongolia, Peking* and *Tibet.*

    2. The names of historical figures who died before the general adoption of Pinyin in 1979 are spelled in their familiar form: *Chiang Kai-shek, Sun Yat-sen, Confucius, Mao Tse-tung, Chou En-lai.*

B. After an initial phase-in period when the old Wade-Giles spelling was given in parentheses after the Pinyin, the current style is to use Pinyin only. For instance:

    1. *Nanjing, Tianjin, Chongqing, Shanghai.*

    2. *Guangdong province, Sichuan province, Heilongjiang province.*

    3. *Deng Xiaoping, Hua Guofeng, Li Xiannian, Jiang Qing.* On second references: *Deng, Hua, Li, Jiang.*

    4. *Qing Dynasty, Ming Dynasty.*

    5. The names of the *Pearl, Yangtze* and *Yellow* rivers are translated in all instances. Names of other Chinese rivers are not translated except for specific purposes.

    The Sino-Soviet border rivers are the *Ussuri* and the *Amur,* despite the Chinese usages of *Wusuli* and *Heilong.*

    6. Note that only the Chinese proper name is used and that the Chinese word for the geographical feature described is translated. Thus it is not *Huaihe* but *Huai River.*

    Some of the Chinese suffixes and their English meanings:

    he, jiang (river); *shan, ling* (mountain); *hu* (lake); *hai* (sea); *yang* (ocean); *dao* (island)

C. The Wade-Giles spellings are used for people and places outside the territory administered by the People's Republic of China, such as Taiwan, Hong Kong and Macao. Thus, in Taiwan, it is *President Chiang Ching-kuo*, and the capital is *Taipei*.

D. Names of overseas Chinese are spelled and punctuated and placed in the order that they prefer: *Prime Minister Lee Kuan Yew* of Singapore.

INDIA

A. Most Indian names follow standard anglicized usages, but three points merit our attention:

1. In South India, most names carry two initials: *V. V. Giri*.

2. The middle initial is generally regarded as an important part of a person's identity: *Morarji R. Desai*. Some, however, have elected to drop it completely: *Jawaharlal Nehru*.

3. Women's names consist of a first name, the initial of her father's first name and the surname: *Indira J. Nehru* is the daughter of the late Jawaharlal Nehru.

   After her marriage, she became *Indira F. Gandhi*, the initial standing for her husband's first name. (Since then, she has, like her father, dispensed with the initial.)

B. The terms *Pandit*, *Maulana* and *Sardar* are commonly used as titles. *Pandit* means scholar, *Maulana* means priest and *Sardar* means nobleman or military officer. They should be capitalized before names and lowercased when standing alone. In many cases they call for definition.

   Pandit is also sometimes a surname: *Mme. Pandit*.

C. The suffix *-ji* is sometimes added to a person's name as a gesture of familiar respect. We should not use it except in direct quotations unless it has become an integral part of the name as is the case with *Morarji R. Desai*.

INDONESIA

A. In most cases use the last element of the name on second reference: *A. H. Nasution, Nasution; Ali Sastroamidjojo, Sastroamidjojo*.

B. Muslim names
1. If a filial indicator such as *bin* appears, use the last element of the name before the indicator as a second reference.
2. If no filial indicator appears, use the last element of the name as a second reference.
3. Names including *Abu* or *Abdul* should use that word plus the word immediately following as a second reference.
4. Some Muslim names include a place name. The element of the name preceding the place name should be used on second reference: *Abdullah Udjong Buloh, Abdullah.* When a name appears to fit this category, check a gazetteer.

IRAN

A. Generally speaking, the final element of the name should be used on second reference: *Mehdi Bazargan, Bazargan.*

B. But some names consist of two two-part elements. Some of these, like *Amin Khosrow Afshar Ghasemlu,* have the appearance of a four-element name, but the appropriate second reference is *Afshar Ghasemlu.* Others may consist of two solid elements or a hyphenated element:

   Sheikul Eslamzadeh, Eslamzadeh; Jaafar Sharif-Emami, Sharif-Emami

C. There is no problem with *el* or *al* or *ul* because in all instances they are merged into another word: *Sheikul Eslamzadeh.*

D. Such filial indicators as *ibn* and *bin* should be lowercased in full names but uppercased when used with the last name only.

E. Authorities differ on the transliteration that can give us either *Abdullah* or *Abdollah, Hussein* or *Hossein.* The Times makes an arbitrary ruling for the *u* sound on the grounds of simplicity:

   Abdullah, Hussein, Nasrullah, Nematullah.

   An exception: *the Ayatollah Ruhollah Khomeini.*

F. The late shah was *Mohammed Reza Pahlavi.*

G. Some names are presented to us as beginning with *Q: Qarabaghi, Qarani.* But the sound is heavily guttural, and The Times uses *Gharabaghi* and *Gharani.* This generally does not apply to place names, in which the *Q* will be retained: *Qom.*

H. Avoid the European-derived diphthongs. Make it *Hakim*, not *Hakeem*. And spell it *Bakhtiar*, not *Bakhtiyar*.

I. Miscellaneous Iranian names: *Nassir, Hassan, Hussein, Ayub, Shahpour, Abdul, Jamshid, Daryush, Hushang, Jaafar, Hoveida, Mohammed, Manuchehr.*

KOREA

Korean names generally consist of a family name followed by a two-element personal name. But there was a time when by official decree the order was reversed to put the family name last. The Times' usage is to follow the traditional order, capitalizing all three elements without any hyphen, except when we know of a personal preference:

Park Chung Hee, Park; Kim Il Sung, Kim; Syngman Rhee, Rhee; Tongsun Park, Park

MALAYSIA

A. One major problem, as in Burma, is that of honorifics, among which are *Datuk, Dato, Tunku, Tun, Tan* and *Tan Sri*.

    1. As in Bangladesh and Burma, we should use only one honorific per person. And we should not use them when another title is used:

        Prime Minister Hussein bin Onn, Datuk Hussein bin Onn, Hussein

    2. Such a title should not be used on second reference except when used generally:

        The tunku went on to say . . . .

B. Surnames are rare in Malaysia, occurring only among Western-oriented people. The entire name should generally be used on second reference.

Major exceptions are found among Chinese names, which follow personal preference, and Muslim names derived from the Arabic, which include a filial indicator. In Malaysia, the customary indicator is *bin* (sometimes *binte*)—in contrast with *ibn* in the Middle East and *ben* in North Africa. In these cases only the name elements preceding the filial indicator should be used on second reference: *Hussein bin Onn, Hussein; Abdul Razak bin Hussein, Abdul Razak.*

Note that *Abdul* in Malaysia does not merge with other names to form compounds like *Abdulaziz*, as it does in the Middle East, but remains separate—except in the case of *Abdullah*.

THAILAND AND LAOS

A. Thais tend to be known by the first name element, even on second reference: *Prapass Charusathira, Prapass.*

B. Thai royal names are actually written as one long Thai word and are broken up only for the convenience of foreigners. They usually consist of seven syllables, and the break usually occurs after the third.

C. Laotian royalty, such as Prince Souvanna Phouma and Prince Souphanouvong should be referred to by the full name on second reference.

D. Most other Laotians should be referred to on second reference by the initial name element:

Premier Kaysone Phomvihan, Kaysone; Kong Le, Kong

VIETNAM

A. In most Vietnamese names, the first name is the family name: Nguyen Van Thieu belongs to the Nguyen family; Ngo Dinh Nhu and Ngo Dinh Diem belonged to the Ngo family.

But there are only 12 major family names, and everyone is referred to by the terminal name element:

Pham Van Dong, Dong; Nguyen Cao Ky, Ky; Tran Van Don, Don

(54% of all Vietnamese are named Nguyen; an additional 31% are named Tran, Le, Pham, Vu, Ngo, Do, Hoang, Dao, Dang, Duong or Dinh.)

B. The late Ho Chi Minh is a special instance. The name is really a *nom de guerre* meaning "He Who Enlightens." The use of *Ho* on second reference is preferred.

as if, as though, like   Both *as if* and *as though* are acceptable conjunctions: *He looked as if he had lost his best friend.*

But the use of *like* as a conjunction, in spite of the cigarette advertising, is generally regarded as substandard and should not be used in The Times except for deliberate colloquial effect or in direct quotations.

assassin, killer, murderer   An *assassin* is a politically motivated killer. A *killer* is anyone who kills, but the term is to be used cautiously, for it suggests one who kills habitually or wantonly. A *murderer* is one who has been convicted of murder.

assault, battery   In a general sense *assault* is used to denote physical contact and sudden violence in an attack. Legally, *assault* denotes merely the threat of violent attack. *Assault and battery* is the legal term used when the assailant actually does touch his victim with his body or a weapon.

assistant   Do not abbreviate when used as a title or part of a title: *Assistant Atty. Gen. Drew S. Days.*

association   Abbreviate when it is the final element in a proper name: *American Medical Assn.* Spell out when it occurs earlier: *the Association of American Railroads.*

assume, presume   In some usages the two words are virtually synonymous. In the sense of inferring something, it may be said that *presume* indicates a strong conviction and *assume* indicates a hypothesis:

Since you went to the bank, I *presume* that you made a deposit. Let's *assume* that you are on one side and I am on the other.

But a primary meaning of *assume* is *to feign*, and here *presume* cannot be a synonym:

He *assumed* a mantle of righteousness when he became a judge. And *assume* cannot be a synonym when *presume* means *take advantage of*:

He *presumed* on the good will of the United States when he set out to crush the rebels.

at about   See about.

at, in   The distinction is a fine one and becoming increasingly blurred. But, in general, use *at* to refer to an exterior location, a general location, or a temporary location. Use *in* to refer to an interior location, a specific location or a more permanent location. But editors and writers must listen to how the phrase sounds and let their consciences be their guides:

He died *at* the hospital.

He died *in* the emergency room *at* the hospital.

He pitched his tent *in* an orchard *at* Victorville.

The march ended *at* Victorville.

They were married *in* St. Matthew's Church.

The right-to-life rally was held *at* St. Matthew's Church; after the rally Mass was said *in* the church. (Rally outside, Mass inside.)

at-bat   Sometimes, in sports parlance, a noun: *He had three at-bats.*

Atlantic Alliance

at present, presently   *At present* means now; *presently* means soon.

attribution   It is preferable to say *Begin said* rather than *said Begin.* Attribution should generally go at the end of a quotation or be inserted at a natural pause.

Avoid the use of words like *smiled* and *frowned* as attributives:

Wrong: *"Hello," he smiled.*

Wrong: *"What's the matter?" she frowned.*

Atty. Gen.   The abbreviation may be used before the name of a person or standing alone in headlines. Such titles as *assistant attorney general* should be abbreviated to *Assistant Atty. Gen.* but these should not stand alone in headlines. It is often preferable for such longer titles to be placed after the name of the holder, lowercased and set off with commas.

The same applies to *Dist. Atty.*

Do not abbreviate *Deputy* or *Assistant* whether they are complete titles or partial ones.

author   Avoid its use as a verb.

auto makers, auto workers, car workers   All two words. See **Unions.**

Ave.   Abbreviate in numbered addresses only: *314 West 6th Ave., Blake and Adams avenues, Madison Avenue.*

averse, adverse   *Averse* means unwilling, disinclined, opposed to. *Adverse* means unfavorable, harmful.

He is averse to hitchhiking through the desert; the aridity, the heat and the intense isolation have an adverse effect on him.

ax   Not *axe.*

Axis   Capitalize in reference to the German-Italian-Japanese alliance in World War II.

B

baby-sit, baby-sitting, baby sitter

backpack, backpacker

back seat The noun is two words; hyphenate the adjective: *back-seat driver.*

backstroke

back to back, back-to-back Hyphenate the adjective, not the *adverb:*
They stood back to back.
They were in a back-to-back position.

backup Both noun and adjective. The verb is two words.

backward Not *backwards.*

backyard One word, both noun and adjective.

Baghdad The capital of Iraq is spelled with an *h*. Other communities, in Arizona, Florida and Mexico, are spelled *Bagdad.*

bail-out Hyphenate both the noun and the adjective, but not the verb.
Congress voted bail-out funds for New York City.
Congress voted a massive bail-out for New York City.
Congress refused to bail out New York City.

ballcarrier, ballclub, ballgame, ballpark, ballplayer But it's *ball handler* and *ball handling.*

ballpoint An exception to Webster's New World Dictionary.

bandanna

44

bar associations It's the *Los Angeles County Bar Assn.* but: *State Bar of California* or *California State Bar.* Usages in other states may vary.

barbell

bar mitzvah Note also the feminine equivalent: *bat mitzvah.*

barrio In Spanish-speaking countries, a district or a suburb of a city. In the United States, an urban district with large numbers of Spanish-speaking residents.

bayonet, bayoneted

BB gun

BC See **AD.**

bedrock

beef Wellington

Bel-Air The name of the residential area takes a hyphen, but many commercial ventures do not and should be checked: *Hotel Bel-Air, Bel Air Sands Hotel.*

belie, belied, belying

belts Geographical belts are always two words: *Sun Belt, Corn Belt, Frost Belt, Wheat Belt.*

Benediction Capitalize the name of the ritual. Lowercase other wise.

benefit, benefited, benefiting

Berlin Wall

best seller, best-selling

between, among Use *between* for two items, *among* for more than two. There are exceptions, but this is a good general rule.

between . . . and . . . Always make it *between this and that,* never *between this to that.*

bi- In general, no hyphen: *bifocal, bilateral, bilingual, bipartisan.*

biannual, biennial *Biannual* means semiannual or twice a year. *Biennial* means every two years. Because of the frequent confusion of these terms, it is wise to avoid them.

Bible Capitalize, without quotation marks, when referring to the Old Testament and/or the New Testament. Also such synonyms as: *the Gospels, the Scriptures, Holy Writ*. But, informally: *the gospel truth; the stylebook is his bible*. Lowercase *biblical*.

Do not abbreviate individual books of the Bible. Numbered books take an Arabic numeral before the name: *2 Samuel*.

Citations citing chapter and verse(s): *Matthew 3:16, 1 Kings 4:9-10*.

Books of the Bible may be casually referred to as *Samuel, Chronicles, Corinthians, Revelation*.

(Do not use the term *Old Testament* in referring to that part of the Bible in a Jewish context.)

Bible Belt Avoid this generally pejorative term.

Bicentennial Capitalize references to the U.S. Bicentennial.

Big Apple Fanciful term for New York City.

Big Board The New York Stock Exchange.

Big Red One The 1st Infantry Division.

Big 10, Big 8 The sports usages.

Big Three, Big Four In the automotive industry.

big time The adjective is *big-time*. Also a *big-timer*.

bills Do not capitalize the names of unpassed legislation: *the national health insurance bill*.

biorhythm

Bird, Rose Elizabeth Use the full name of the chief justice of California on first reference.

bishop Capitalize before a person's name: *Bishop James Webb; James Webb, bishop of Santa Cruz; the bishop of Santa Cruz*.

Two exceptions: *the Archbishop of Canterbury, the Archbishop of York.*

See also **Religious References.**

bitter, bitters *Bitter* is the strongly hopped British ale: *a pint of bitter. Bitters* is the highly herbed flavoring used in some cocktails, soups and sauces: *Angostura bitters, gin and bitters.*

black Generally preferred to *Negro, colored person* or other similar terms except when the others are parts of a proper name: *Negro Labor Committee, National Association for the Advancement of Colored People.* See **Ethnic Designations.**

Black Caucus

Black Power

blame It is preferable to *blame someone for something* than to *blame something on someone.* But the latter is permissible.

Blessed Sacrament

Blessed Virgin

blizzard Wind speeds of 35 m.p.h. or higher and considerable falling or blowing of snow with visibility near zero.

A severe blizzard involves 45-m.p.h. wind speeds or higher, great density of falling snow with visibility near zero and temperature of 10 degrees or lower.

bloc A bloc is a political grouping or a pressure group, such as *the farm bloc.*

blond, brunet The feminine versions of these terms are *blonde* and *brunette.* They should be applied to women only when the physical description is necessary to the story. Hair of people of either sex should be described as *blond* or *brunet.* See also **Courtesy Titles and Sex References.**

Bloody Mary

blowup The noun and the adjective. The verb is two words: *Don't blow up at me.*

blue blood A person may have *blue blood,* be *blue-blooded* or be a *blueblood.*

blue-ribbon Hyphenate the adjective: *blue-ribbon grand jury.*

Blvd. Abbreviate in numbered addresses only.

B'nai B'rith

Board of Education In some communities it is the Board of Education; in others it is the School Board. In Los Angeles: the *Los Angeles Board of Education* except when confusion is possible and *Los Angeles City Board of Education* is used. Also: *Los Angeles school board, Los Angeles city school board.*

boat Generally speaking a *boat* is a vessel that can be taken on board a *ship,* such as a lifeboat. Some exceptions: *PT boat, ferryboat, U-boat, gunboat.*

bogeys, bogeyed In golf.

bona fide Two words. No hyphen, no italics.

boo-boo

booby trap Two words. Hyphenate verb and adjective.

book titles See **Arts and Letters.**

borderline Both noun and adjective.

"born-again" Lowercase, with quotation marks and hyphen, as an adjective to describe those Christians whose faith has been renewed by a moment of religious insight or experience: *a "born-again" Christian.*

Do not use hyphen if used as a verb: *President Carter has been "born again."*

Do not use *reborn* as a synonym in the religious usage.

borscht Spelling an exception to Webster's New World Dictionary.

box office Hyphenate the adjective: *a box-office attraction.*

boyfriend

boy, youth, man *Boy* is applicable through the age of 17. *Youth* is applicable to boys 13 through 17. *Young man* or *man* is applicable from the age of 18 on.

the Boy Scouts, a Boy Scout, the Scouts, a Scout The organization and its members.

Bradley, Tom See **mayors.**

Brahma, Brahman, Brahmin *Brahma* is a species of domestic fowl. *Brahman* is a caste of Indian society or a breed of cattle. *Brahmin* is a term for aristocracy in general: *a Boston Brahmin.*

brand-new

break Use this layman's term to describe simple bone fractures, but *fracture* may be used when more technical terminology is necessary: *a greenstick fracture, a compound fracture.*

breaststroke

the Bronx Note the lowercase article.

Brother Capitalize when used as a title before a name. Roman Catholic brothers and sisters are not members of the clergy. *Brother* or *Sister* may be used on second reference if the person has only one name: *Brother Antoninus.*

Brown, Edmund G., Jr. See **governors.**

brush fire The noun is two words. The adjective is *brush-fire.*

brushoff The noun. The verb is two words.

BTU, BTUs British thermal unit. Abbreviation acceptable on second reference.

bulletproof

bull's-eye

bumper to bumper The adverb. Hyphenate the adjective.

burglary, robbery, theft In general, burglary is the act of breaking into a building to commit a theft or other crime. *Theft* includes larceny, embezzlement and stealing. *Robbery* is theft that involves the use of violence or the threat of violence and occurs in presence of the victim.

A bandit *robs* a person, a bank or a liquor store but *steals* money or jewels.

These definitions are based on California law. They may differ in other jurisdictions.

burned, burnt   In general use *burned* as the past tense or past participle. But *burnt* should be used in certain instances: *burnt offering, burnt sienna*.

bus, bused, busing   Referring to transportation.

buss, bussed, bussing   Referring to kissing.

buzz saw

by-   In general no hyphen: *bylaw, byplay, bystander*. An exception: *by-election*.

Bylines

These rules apply to the Los Angeles Times. Other papers, of course, have styles of their own.

   I. In general bylines should be set in nine-point type, capitalized and centered, with appropriate identification centered in six-point bold below it. Note the lowercase *y* in *by*.

By JACK JONES
Times Staff Writer

   II. Staffers who use an article or a preposition as a surname prefix should have the prefix lowercased if this is their preference:

By FRANK del OLMO
Times Staff Writer

By PENELOPE McMILLAN
Times Staff Writer

By A. KENT MacDOUGALL
Times Staff Writer

By DOROTHY VANDERVELD
Times Staff Writer

III. In double bylines the *and* should be lowercased:

By JACK JONES and FRANK del OLMO
Times Staff Writers

When such a byline has to run over into a second line, the word *and* should be placed on that second line.

IV. Bylines of other writers should be handled similarly:

By NICHOLAS von HOFFMAN
The Washington Post

By KAREN DeYOUNG
The Washington Post

By LaBARBARA BOWMAN
The Washington Post

By HUGH MULLIGAN
Associated Press

By JACK FOX
United Press International

(In the case of the Associated Press and United Press International, the parenthetical credit should be eliminated in favor of the six-point line when a byline is used.)

V. When the use of a staffer's byline is not desired, the phrase From a Times Staff Writer, in six-point bold, may be substituted.

VI. In instances in which the staffer already has one byline on the same page, an accompanying story may be credited by putting the writer's name in ninepoint light, flush right, all capitals, on a separate line at the end of a story.

VII. The phrase Special to The Times, in six-point bold, should be used with such special material as the Gallup Poll or free-lance work.

VIII. Stories without bylines that originate with other publications and wire service stories that have no dateline or logotype should be credited with a six-point bold line only:

From Associated Press
From United Press International
From Agence France-Presse
From Reuters
From Newhouse News Service
From the Chicago Sun-Times
From the Congressional Quarterly
From the Financial Times of London
From the Observer
From the Guardian
From the Washington Post
From the Dallas Times Herald
From Newsday

IX. The phrase From Times Wire Services, in six-point bold, should be used when a story has been put together from a number of sources.

X. Stories by free-lancers take no identification line. Such identification, in greater detail, should be made in a box insert or at the end of a story. Always use a box insert in main section news stories.

C

Cabinet Capitalize when referring to the specific cabinet of a specific country: *the U.S. Cabinet, the Cabinet, the French Cabinet.*

Lowercase plurals and general uses: *the cabinets of Britain and France; a cabinet.*

cactus The plural is *cacti.*

Caesarean Capitalize.

Caesars Palace No apostrophe.

Caltech Acceptable in The Times in all instances.

Caltrans Acceptable both in Times headlines and text. Always include one complete version in the text: *California Department of Transportation.*

cancel out A redundancy. Make it *cancel.*

canister Not *cannister.*

can opener

capital, Capitol The *capital* is the city, the *Capitol* the building.

Capitalization

    I. The Times has a modified up-style of capitalization. These basic rules apply:

        A. Capitalize proper names.

        B. Capitalize titles in front of names.

        C. Lowercase plurals and general and generic references.

        D. Lowercase when uncertain.

II. Refer to Webster's New World Dictionary for capitalization of words or phrases not covered here or in other entries in this book. The dictionary may indicate capitalization "usually," "often," "occasionally" or "also." The Times capitalizes when the reference says "usually" or "often."

III. Capitalization of arts and letters terms is covered under **Arts and Letters.**

IV. Papers, programs, pacts and laws

A. Capitalize documents and doctrines, enacted laws, ratified treaties and constitutional amendments:

Constitution (U.S. or state), Magna Charta, Marshall Plan, National Labor Relations Act, Taft-Hartley Act, Truman Doctrine, U.N. Charter, 18th Amendment

B. Lowercase pending or defeated legislation, general references and plurals:

equal rights amendment, nuclear accords, tax reform bill, Truman and Monroe doctrines

V. Geographical areas

A. Capitalize geographical or descriptive names of regions:

the Antarctic; the Central Highlands (of Vietnam); *East Coast, Gulf Coast, West Coast* (of the United States); *Eastern Seaboard; Eastern Shore* (of Maryland or Virginia); *the Great Plains; the High Sierra, the Sierra; the Left Bank* (of the Seine); *the Loop* (in Chicago); *Lower East Side* (of New York); *the Maritime Provinces* (of Canada); *the Middle East; the Midwest; the North, the South, the West* (in the United States); *the Panhandle; South-Central Los Angeles; Southern California; the Southern Tier* (of New York state); *Upstate New York; the West Bank* (of the Jordan)

Do not capitalize areas not generally recognized as specific regions: *southern Arkansas, western Connecticut*

B. Capitalize major natural features and fanciful geographic appellations:

Continental Divide, Corn Belt, Deep South, Down East (Maine), *Down Under, Emperor Seamount Chain, Gulf Stream, Ho Chi Minh Trail, Los Angeles Basin, the Lower 48, Mindanao Deep, Pikes Peak, San Andreas Fault, Sun Belt*

Do not capitalize the word *state: Washington state, New York state*

C. Capitalize such artificial designations as:

the Equator, International Date Line, the Mason-Dixon Line, the North Temperate Zone, the South Pole, the 17th Parallel

D. Capitalize *Occidental, Orient, Oriental.*

E. Lowercase generic terms standing by themselves unless they are used in a specific sense:

the altiplano, the coast, the desert, the high desert, the hemisphere, the mountains

But:

the Islands (Hawaii); *the Continent* (Europe); *the States* (the United States); *the Street* (Wall Street)

Note that the United States, without Alaska or Hawaii, is the *contiguous United States,* not the *continental.*

G. Lowercase most plurals: *Orange and San Diego counties, Main and 3rd streets*

VI. Government bodies of all kinds

A. Proper or generally accepted names, including certain short forms:

(U.N.) Security Council, State Department, the Presidium, the Knesset, the Cortes, the Bundestag, the Politburo, British Embassy, French Consulate, Foreign Service, Secret Service, state Legislature, City Council, L.A. Police Department, Police Department (avoid such usages as *LAPD* and *USDA*), *L.A. County Jail*

B. Temporary bodies but not proposed ones:

Warren Commission, (House) Ethics Committee, (Senate) Watergate Committee, International Control Commission

But: *the proposed department of consumer affairs*

C. Informal terms. But make sure the terms are defined somewhere in the story:

the Fed, the Hill, Fannie Mae

D. Internal elements should be lowercased unless they are clearly identifiable without reference to their parent bodies:

the civil rights division of the Department of Justice

But:

the Federal Bureau of Investigation, the Immigration and Naturalization Service, the Bureau of Land Management

E. Lowercase generic references standing alone:

the board, the bureau, the agency, the embassy

F. Lowercase plurals:

the 18th and 19th amendments
the departments of Labor and the Interior

G. Lowercase informal terms:

the high court, the judiciary, the executive branch, the lower house, the post office, the weather bureau

But: *the Administration*

H. Capitalize names of government committees, but lowercase names of subcommittees unless they have acquired generally accepted identities of their own.

Senate Judiciary Committee, Senate Judiciary subcommittee on court reform, Senate subcommittee on court reform

I. Lowercase such words as *city, state, federal* and *national* except when they are part of the full title of a body or in formal reference to the legal entity:

The City of Los Angeles filed suit today . . ., *the city Department of Water and Power, the state Water Project*

When doubt exists, these titles should be checked in the California Roster, the Congressional Quarterly and similar references.

J. Capitalize parenthetical translations as appropriate:

Bundestag (lower house of Parliament) Gush Emunim (Faith Bloc)

K. Capitalize names of programs and agencies but not concepts:

Social Security payments, Civil Service tests, Selective Service director, Social Security Administration

But: *the idea of social security, the purpose of selective service, civil service principles*

VII. Capitalize names of buildings, rooms, bridges, parks, etc.:

Berlin Wall, Bradbury Building, the Capitol (the building), *City Hall* (as an informal term for city government or a specific building), *Death Row, East Room* (of the White House), *Empire State Building, Little Tokyo, MacArthur Park, Old City* (of Jerusalem), *Peripheral Canal, Pershing Square, Piccadilly Circus, Red Square* (in Moscow), *Santa Ana Freeway, Skid Row* (*Skid Road* in the Pacific Northwest), *Tower of London, Vincent Thomas Bridge, Western Wall* (in Jerusalem, not *Wailing Wall*)

Lowercase similar words used generically or in plurals.

VIII. Military usages

A. Capitalize full and short forms of U.S. services but only full and specific names of foreign ones. Lowercase plurals and generic references:

U.S. Navy, the Army, Marine Corps, the Marines, National Guard, Air Force Reserve, French Foreign Legion, French army, Royal Air Force, British air force, People's Liberation Army

B. Capitalize specific bases, commands, schools and ships:

Vandenberg Air Force Base, Ft. Ord, Camp Pendleton, Joint Chiefs of Staff, 6th Fleet, Atlantic Fleet, German General Staff, Sierra Army Depot, Corps of Engineers, Rocky Mountain Arsenal, U.S. Naval Academy, the aircraft carrier Nimitz

Note: Do not use *USS* or *HMS* in front of names of naval vessels except in datelines. Make it *the U.S. aircraft carrier Nimitz, the aircraft carrier Nimitz* or *the carrier Nimitz,* as appropriate.

C. Capitalize official names of units:

39th Infantry Regiment (or 39th Infantry), the 23rd Marines, Company A, 1st Battalion, 9th Infantry Division, 3rd Marine Division, 3rd Armored Division, 395th Artillery

D. Capitalize fanciful names for units:

Green Berets, Afrika Korps, Fighting 69th, Big Red One, Rainbow Division, Red Army

E. Capitalize rank preceding a name:

Col. William R. Corson

F. Capitalize names of wars, major battles, revolts and military or "police" actions, regardless of whether war has actually been declared or not:

World War II, French Revolution, the Battle of San Juan Hill, Civil War (English, Spanish or U.S.), *Boxer Rebellion, Hundred Years' War, Boer War, Russian* (or *October* or *Bolshevik*) *Revolution, the Battle of the Bulge, the Six-Day War, the Vietnam War, the Korean War, the Yom Kippur War, the Cold War*

G. Lowercase *soldier, sailor, airman, paratrooper.*

Capitalize *National Guardsman, Coast Guardsman, Green Beret, Marine.*

Lowercase *naval officer, guardsman, legionnaire.*

IX. Politics and parties

A. Capitalize political organizations, tendencies and movements:

Democratic Party, Republican Party, Peace and Freedom Party, Young Democrats, New Left, Communists, a Socialist, Black Caucus, Black Power, National Liberation Front, Provisional wing (Provos) of the Irish Republican Army

B. Conventions, their chief bodies and titles before names of their chief officers should be capitalized.

Republican National Convention, Democratic Platform Committee, Communist Central Committee, Republican National Chairman Bill Brock

C. Capitalize fanciful appellations:

Solid South, Great Society, Fair Deal, New Deal, Old Guard, Young Turks, Reds, New Freedom, Whip Inflation Now (WIN)

But: *hawks, doves, hawkish, dovish*

D. Capitalize party members and adherents (as distinct from a philosophy and its adherents):

Democrats, Laborites, Christian Democrats, Communists

E. Political philosophies and forms of government should be lowercased:

democratic principles, republican system, right-winger, leftist, left wing, communism, a communist theory, a communist nation, a communist movement

But: *a Marxist philosopher*

It is important to bear in mind the distinction here: When referring to a specific party or its members, capitalize; when referring to a political philosophy, lowercase.

X. Political groupings

A. Capitalize specific government bodies:

Los Angeles County Board of Supervisors, Board of Supervisors, Borough of Manhattan, Crown colony, City Council, state Legislature, Cabinet (U.S. or otherwise)

But: *Washington state, New York state, Quebec province, the board, the supervisors, the council*

B. Capitalize formal and informal names of alliances, blocs, treaties and similar groupings:

East and West (in Europe), *the Allies* (in both world wars), *the Axis* (in World War II), *the Common Market, the Treaty of Rome, the Atlantic Alliance*

But: *the NATO nations, the Warsaw Pact powers, the Eastern Bloc, the Western Bloc*

C. Capitalize political districts:

43rd Assembly District, 24th Congressional District

D. Capitalize popular appellations:

Bamboo Curtain, Berlin Wall, Free World, Iron Curtain, Third World

Free World should be used only in direct quotations.

XI. Proper names

A. Capitalize corporations and unions but lowercase articles and general references:

General Motors Corp., Penn Central, Teamsters Union, the Teamsters, the Newspaper Guild, the guild, United Auto Workers, the auto workers, the company, the union

B. Civic and social groups

the American Legion, a legionnaire; B'nai B'rith; the Boy Scouts, a Boy Scout, a Scout; an Elk; the Knights of Pythias; Ku Klux Klan, the klan, a klansman, the kleagle (but *Kleagle John Y. Smith*); *Little League, Little Leaguer; Odd Fellows, an Odd Fellow*

C. Historic events and periods

the Cultural Revolution (in China); *the Dark Ages; the (Great) Depression; the Elizabethan Age; the Great Leap Forward* (in China); *the Industrial Revolution; the Jazz Age; the Renaissance; Revolutionary times* (referring to the American Revolution); *the Space Age; the Stone Age*

D. Speeches

Gettysburg Address, Roosevelt's fireside chats, Speech From the Throne, State of the Union message (but *budget message*), *Washington's Farewell Address*

E. Holidays and celebrations

Election Day, Father's Day, the Fourth of July, Inauguration Day, Independence Day, Mardi Gras, Mother's Day, New Year's Day (New Year's Eve, New Year's, the new year), Tet, U.S. Bicentennial, the Bicentennial, Valentine's Day, Veterans Day

F. Major sports events and trophies

Americas Cup (golf), *America's Cup* (yachting), *Davis Cup, Olympic Games (the Olympics, the Games), the British Open, Rose Bowl, Super Bowl, World Cup, World Series*

G. Schools, colleges and universities

1. For usage on state colleges and universities and for further details see **Academic Usages.**

2. In general capitalize all full names of schools, colleges and universities and many abbreviated forms:

   Harvard University, Harvard College; Hollywood High School, Hollywood High; The Buckley School; Robert F. Kennedy Elementary School, Kennedy Elementary, Kennedy School; 95th St. Elementary School; St. Michael's High, St. Michael's

3. Names of divisions larger than an academic department and names of graduate schools and professional schools connected with a college or university are capitalized:

UCLA Law School, USC Law Center, Harvard Dental School

4. Names of departments are generally lowercased: *the physics department, the English department*

H. Honors and decorations

Medal of Honor (not *Congressional*), *Distinguished Service Cross, Order of the British Empire, Purple Heart, Good Conduct Medal, Nobel Prize, Nobel Peace Prize, Nobel Prize for chemistry, Most Valuable Player Award* (if a specific one), *Phi Beta Kappa, Heisman Trophy*

But: *Olympic gold medal, magna cum laude, battlefield citation*

I. Races and ethnic groups

Anglo, Asian, Caucasian, Chicano, Latin, Latino, Oriental

Also: *Colored* (when referring to South Africa)

And: *white, black, yellow, brown*

See also **Ethnic Designations.**

J. Popular appellations:

the Big Apple, the Big Board, the Big Three auto makers, the Black Dahlia, the City of the Angels, Death Row, Dixie, the Empire State, the Fourth Estate, the Gang of Four, the Golden State, Hurricane Connie, the Lower 48, the Old Dominion, the Skid Row Slasher, the Southland (Southern California), *the Stars and Stripes, the Union, the Union Jack, the Windy City, ZIP code*

K. Proper names that have acquired independent meanings are sometimes lowercased, sometimes capitalized. Check Webster's New World Dictionary for specific cases other than the following:

portland cement, manhattan cocktail, navy blue, french fries, napoleon (pastry), *quisling*

But: *Paris green, Oxford gray, Molotov cocktail, Chinese red, French cuff, Oriental rug, Diesel engine, Gatling gun, Swiss cheese, Bermuda shorts, Gestapo tactics*

XII. Religion. See **Religious References.**

XIII. Capitalize names of planets, constellations and other astronomical features. Capitalize *Earth* in its context as a planet but not in its general use.

Capitalize: *Martian, Venusian;* lowercase: *sun, moon, stars.* Note: *Halley's comet.*

XIV. Titles

    A. Titles indicating position or status (as opposed to job description) should be capitalized when they precede names.

    President Carter, First Lady Rosalynn Carter, School Supt. William Johnston, Ambassador-at-Large David Rockefeller, County Supervisor Pete Schabarum, (City) Councilman Joel P. Wachs, NFL Commissioner Pete Rozelle, Arkansas Coach Lou Holtz (but not line coach, assistant coach, defensive coach, first-base coach or positions on a team), *Cubs Manager Herman Franks, Heublein Chairman Stuart D. Watson, Times Editor William F. Thomas, Times Publisher Tom Johnson*

    B. Academic, military, professional, quasi-military, religious or royal titles should be capitalized when they immediately precede names:

    Prof. Herbert Marcuse, Col. William R. Corson, Police Lt. Walter Page, Pope John Paul II, Queen Elizabeth II

    C. Capitalize formal terms of protocol:

    Your Majesty, His Royal Highness, Your Honor, His Excellency

    D. Popular appellations should be capitalized—both before a name and standing alone:

    King of Swing Benny Goodman; Benny Goodman, the King of Swing; Defender of the Faith; the Brown Bomber

    E. Lowercase most titles when they stand alone, except when such a title to some extent constitutes the person's name:

    the senator, the chairman, the Speaker (of the House),

the Dalai Lama, the Duke of Somerset, the duke, the Pope

See also **Nobility and Royalty.**

Exceptions: *the President, the First Lady* (of the United States; the same applies to *First Family* and *Royal Family*)

Capitalize *Vice President* only before a name.

F. Capitalize *House Majority Leader* and *Senate Minority Leader* before names. But when the title is an informal one, make it *House Democratic leader* and *Senate Republican leader*.

G. Lowercase plural and general terms, derivatives and qualifying terms:

the councilmen; the presidential race; the presidency; the ex-President, acting Police Chief Robert F. Rock, then-Police Chief Ed Davis

H. Do not capitalize descriptions, such as *film star Robert Redford* or *telephone operator Beatrice Washington.*

I. Do not capitalize temporary or minor titles: *shop steward William Bailey, presidential assistant Homer Lewis, administrative assistant Lisa Ayala, foreman Ernest L. Wood.*

J. Long, unwieldy titles should be placed after the person's name, and lowercased when appropriate: *J. Brian Atwood, deputy assistant of state for congressional relations.*

XV. Capitalize all trade names but use them only when they are necessary to the story or in direct quotations. When the trade name is not necessary, use a generic substitute when feasible. Many trade names can be found in the Trade Names Dictionary (Gale Research). Some of the more common ones:

Alka-Seltzer—antacid tablets
Baggies—plastic bags
Band-Aid—bandage
ChapStick—lip salve

Chiclets—chewing gum
Coca-Cola, Coke—cola drink
Dacron—synthetic fiber
Deepfreeze—home freezer
Dictaphone—dictating machine
Dixie cups—paper cups
Dramamine—travel sickness medicine
Fiberglas—fiber glass
Formica—laminated plastic
Frigidaire—refrigerator
Jell-O—gelatin dessert
Kleenex—tissues
Laundromat—self-service laundry
Levi's—jeans
Mace—tear gas spray
Masonite—hardboard
Mixmaster—food mixer
Novocaine—painkiller
Plexiglas—acrylic plastic
Ping-Pong—table tennis
Polaroid—camera or self-developing film
Quaaludes—tranquilizers
Q-tips—cotton swabs
Saran Wrap—plastic wrap
Scotch tape—cellophane or plastic tape
Sheetrock—gypsum wallboard
Simoniz—car wax
Tabasco—pepper sauce
Technicolor—color movies
TelePrompTer—cuing device
Tommy gun—submachine gun
Vaseline—petroleum jelly
Windbreaker—sports jacket
Xerox—photo copier

XVI. Miscellaneous

    A. Designation terms before figures and letters should be capitalized.

Chapter 9, No. 3, Page 15, Room 212, Route 66, Vitamin C

B. Capitalize initials and all letters of true acronyms, but capitalize only the first letters of acronyms consisting of more than initials:

AFL-CIO, AT&T, CIA, UNESCO, NOW, COYOTE
But: *Geico, Amvets, Euratom, Amtrak*

Note that *NOW* is an acronym for National Organization *for* Women, not *of.*

C. Capitalize the genus, but not the species, in scientific terms for plants, animals, insects or microorganisms:

Tyrannosaurus rex, Aedes aegypti, Thea japonica, Staphylococcus aureus

On second reference: *T. rex, A. aegypti, T. japonica, S. aureus*

Latin terms of this kind should be italicized.
See also **Italics.**

D. Capitalize personifications for special effects:
Mother Nature, Father Time, grim-visaged War

E. Lowercase such terms as *balance of payments, consumer price index, gross national product, liquefied natural gas.*
Some of these are known by capitalized initials, which may be used in headlines or on second reference:

GNP, LNG

F. Lowercase names of seasons and the term *daylight-saving time,* but capitalize *Eastern Daylight Time, Pacific Standard Time.*

G. Capitalize all parts of anglicized surnames unless another preference is known:

Fiorello La Guardia, Lee Kuan Yew

But, in foreign names, the articles and filial references are usually lowercase unless the surname is used alone:

Charles de Gaulle, De Gaulle; Ahmed ben Bella, Ben Bella

See also entries on foreign names, such as **Arabic Names.**

H. Capitalize first letters of complete sentences following a colon, but lowercase phrases following a colon.

But single words following a colon may sometimes be capitalized for emphasis or special effect:

There is only one alternative: War.

See also **Punctuation.**

XVII. Internal elements

A. Use lowercase for internal elements of organizations when they have names that are widely used generic terms:

the board of directors of Times Mirror Co.; the board of trustees of Columbia University; the history department of USC; the sports department of The Times

B. Capitalize internal elements when they have less commonly used names:

the Board of Overseers of Harvard University; the Board of Regents of the University of California; the House of Delegates of the American Medical Assn.; the House of Bishops and the House of Deputies of the Episcopal Church

See also Part VI of this entry and **Academic References.**

Captions and Credits

I. These usages are those of the Los Angeles Times; other publications have widely varying approaches.

II. Photo credits:

A. With Associated Press pictures use the six-point light line, Associated Press photo, flush right. But use the line AP photo when the picture is only one-column.

B. With staff pictures use the eight-point bold line **Times photo by Cal Montney** (or whoever the photographer may be), flush right. But just use Times photo, six-point light, when the picture is only one-column. Full credit may be given when the picture is of unusual quality.

C. With maps or drawings use the eight-point bold line **Times map** (or drawing) **by Don Clement** (or whoever the artist may be), flush right. When individual credit is not desired, use Times map, six-point light.

D. Use the following designation for photos by free-lancers:
Photo for The Times by James E. Freelancer
(eight-point bold)

E. Copyrighted pictures should carry the line:
Photo copyright 1979 by James E. Freelancer
(eight-point bold)

F. Photos from other sources should carry such a designation as:
Washington Post photo (six-point light)

G. Credits for picture layouts, inside a Benday box, for instance, should not exceed the 10-point size of the captions themselves.

III. Caption format

A. Captions should be set 10-point light except in rare instances. A bold cap bar-line or kicker should generally be used in accordance with current usage.

B. Captions for pictures standing alone should be as long as necessary to tell the story. Captions of more than one line and extending more than two columns should be divided into columns in accordance with existing caption forms.

C. The presence of a copy block or similar device does not eliminate the need for individual captions under individual pictures.

D. One-column maps showing the location of a place in the news may often omit the caption. Sometimes, however, such a label as *Where ship went down* is both desirable and effective.

IV. Caption writing

A. Captions in general should consist of complete sentences and should be written in the present tense. Participial phrases constituting the entire caption should be avoided.

In those rare instances in which a caption does consist of such a phrase, it should not end with a period. For instance

Where murder occurred

or

Meeting the press

B. Captions under pictures portraying historical persons or events may be written in the past tense.

C. Some captions that are linked closely with related copy in the layout and consist of only one line may omit the bar-line.

D. Identifications of individuals in pictures should be set off from their names by commas:

John A. Smith, left, and James F. Jones shake . . .
William E. Jackson, in light coat, shakes hands with . . .
Sen. Alan Cranston (D-Calif.), left, welcomes . . .

E. Such identifications are clearly unnecessary when a glance at a picture makes the identifications clear:

Billy Jones, 4, talks to Santa Claus at . . .
President Carter greets Muhammad Ali with . . .

F. Quotations in captions should be enclosed in double quotation marks when they are in the body of the caption and in single quotation marks when they are in the bar-line.

V. These are general guidelines only.

carat, caret, karat A *carat* is a unit of weight for precious stones; a *caret* is a proofreader's mark; a *karat* is a measure of gold content.

CARE Acceptable in all references to Cooperative for American Relief Everywhere: *a CARE package.*

careen, career *Careen* means to lurch or reel while moving rapidly. *Career* as a noun is a profession or lifework. Do not use to mean to move at full speed.

car pool The noun. Hyphenate the verb or the adjective.
We have a car pool.
We are car-pooling every day.

carry over   The verb. The noun is *carry-over*.

casebook

casehardened

caseload

caseworker

catalogue, catalogued, cataloguing

catchall   Adjective or noun.

catholic   Use *Roman Catholic* for a body accepting papal authority. Later references may be condensed to *Catholic*, but the word
Roman should be retained if contrast with other Catholic bodies
is desired.
Lowercase *catholic* in the sense of general or universal.

cave in, cave-in   The verb and the noun.

celebrant, celebrator   A *celebrant* is a participant in a ritual. A
celebrator is just having a good time.

cellblock   One word

Celsius   Use this term rather than *centigrade* for the metric temperature scale. To convert to Fahrenheit, multiply a Celsius
reading by nine, divide by five and add 32. When giving a Celsius
temperature, use: *40 degrees Celsius*; on second reference: *40C*.

center around   Don't use it. Use *center on* or *revolve around*.

center field, center fielder

centigrade   See **Celsius.**

Central Committee   Capitalize in referring to a specific body.

cents   In general, spell out. The symbol ¢ is permissible with
figures in headlines.

century   Capitalize references to specific centuries: *20th Century,
20th-Century politics, 1st Century.*

CETA The Comprehensive Employment and Training Act. CETA is acceptable on second reference and in headlines. Note the *and* in the full title.

chairlift

chairman Capitalize before a name: *Chairman John Smith; committee Chairman John Smith; John Smith, chairman.*

channels See **TV channels.**

charismatic Lowercase except in proper names to designate the movement among Protestant and Catholic groups that stresses emotional expression, "speaking in tongues" and healing. Members of such movements are sometimes referred to as *neo-Pentecostals.*

check mark May be used instead of a dash for special stylistic effect to indicate items in a series.

Chicana, Chicano Generally accepted terms for Mexican-Americans. Do not use any such term unless the ethnic background is relevant. A *Chicana* is a woman, a *Chicano* a man. See also **Ethnic Designations.**

chief justice Capitalize before the name of a person.

children The first name is the appropriate second reference for anyone under 18: *Amy Carter, Amy.*

A courtesy title may be used for special stylistic effect.

Childrens Hospital In Los Angeles, no apostrophe. The usage may vary elsewhere.

China Use only for the People's Republic of China. Do not use *Red China.* The "other China" is *Taiwan.*

Chinese names See **Asian Names.**

chuckhole

church Capitalize in the proper name of a building, a congregation or a denomination: *St. Matthew's Church, the Roman Catholic Church.*

But lowercase when standing alone or in general references: *church policy, two churches, the church.*

See also **Religious References.**

CIA   Acceptable in all instances for the Central Intelligence Agency.

cigarette   Not *cigaret.*

Cinco de Mayo   This Mexican holiday (May 5) is not the Mexican independence day. It is the anniversary of the Battle of Puebla in 1862 when the Mexican army defeated the French invaders. Mexico's independence day falls on Sept. 16, when Miguel Hidalgo y Costilla issued *El Grito de Dolores* in 1810. Cinco de Mayo is celebrated in memory of the 1862 victory.

cities and towns   Use full names except in direct quotations or in headlines:

Las Vegas, but *"we're going to Vegas."*
Los Angeles, but *"we're going to L.A."*
Philadelphia, but *"we're going to Philly."*

Vegas, L.A. and *N.Y.* are acceptable in headlines. Avoid *Philly.*

citizen, resident, national, native, subject   A *citizen* is one who has acquired the full civil rights of a nation either by birth or naturalization. Use *resident,* not *citizen,* in referring to inhabitants of states and cities.

Use *subject* when the government is headed by a sovereign: *a British subject; an American citizen.*

Use *national* to refer to a person residing away from the nation of which he is a citizen or holds a passport.

Use *native* for a person born in a specified location.

citizens band   No apostrophe, lowercase. *CB* is acceptable in heads or on second reference.

the City   The financial district of London. Also known as Threadneedle Street.

City Hall Capitalize when used as a synonym for city government or to refer to a specific building. Lowercase more general references.

He cleared it with City Hall.
He was well-known at City Hall.
He walked over to City Hall.
He built a new city hall at Petaluma.

City of Commerce Capitalize. Also: *City of Industry*.

Civil Service Capitalize references to the official system: *U.S. Civil Service, Civil Service regulations.*

Lowercase general references: *the idea of civil service, civil service principles.*

claim Do not use for *assert*. It carries a connotation of untruth.

class action When referring to a suit filed by an individual or a group on behalf of unnamed and often unidentifiable persons, it is better to call it a *class-action suit*. (Note the hyphen.)

clean and jerk Do not hyphenate when used as a noun.

clean-cut

clean-shaven

clear-cut

clergy Usually a plural noun taking a plural verb: *The clergy are divided on the abortion issue; the clergy were persecuted.*

Members of the Roman Catholic clergy are referred to on first reference as *Father, Msgr., Bishop* or *Archbishop*. Most members of the Protestant clergy use *the Rev.* or *Bishop*. Rabbis use *Rabbi*. See also **Religious References.**

cloture The parliamentary term. Not *closure*.

cloud-seed The verb.

clubhouse

Cmdr., Lt. Cmdr.   Not *Comdr.* or *Lt. Comdr.*

co-   Hyphenate when *co-* means *associate:*
co-author, co-belligerent, co-chairman, co-conspirator, co-defendant, co-host, co-pilot, co-respondent, co-signer, co-star, co-trustee, co-worker
(*Co-ed* is also hyphenated but is to be avoided.)
Do not hyphenate other usages:
coexist, cooperate, coordinate, coerce
An exception: *co-op*

Coach   Capitalize before a name. But do not capitalize *assistant coach, line coach* or team positions.

coal field(s)   Two words.

coast   Lowercase when referring to the physical shoreline: *fishing along the Atlantic coast, oil fields off the west coast.*
Capitalize when referring to regions of the United States lying along the shorelines: *politics of the West Coast, residents of the Gulf Coast, the East Coast elite.*
Do not capitalize smaller entities: *the California coast.*

co-ed   Hyphenate, but avoid when possible.

Coke   Capitalize this trade name for Coca-Cola.

Cold War   Capitalize when referring to the rivalry between the United States and the Soviet Union.

collectable, collectible   Dictionaries differ on the preferred spelling of the adjective and make no reference to the current use as a noun for items that may be collected. Arbitrarily, The Times has decided on *collectable* as the adjective and *collectible* as the noun.

collective nouns   See **Agreement of Subject and Verb.**

collectors' item   Note position of apostrophe.

collide, collision A collision must involve moving objects.
Right: *Two cars collided on Broadway.*
Wrong: *The car collided with a lamppost.*

colon See **Punctuation.**

Colonial Capitalize when referring to the 13 Colonies:
Colonial times, Colonial forces, Colonial architecture
Otherwise, lowercase: *British colonialism; the colonial attitude*

colorblind

Colored Capitalize the South African ethnic group.

combat, combatted, combatting

Comecon The Council for Mutual Economic Assistance comprises the Soviet Union, Poland, Czechoslovakia, East Germany, Hungary, Romania, Cuba, Bulgaria and Mongolia.

comma See **Punctuation.**

Commerce, City of Capitalize.

committee Capitalize when part of a formal name: *House Judiciary Committee.*
Capitalize also when part of an informal but generally accepted name: *Senate Watergate Committee, House Ethics Committee.*
See **subcommittee.**

the Common Market Capitalize.

Communion Capitalize the name of the sacrament. Also: *Holy Communion.*

communism The name of a political philosophy. Lowercase.

Communist Capitalize when referring to the Communist Party of any nation or its members. Lowercase in reference to the philosophy and its adherents.
He is a Communist and he carries a party card.
Philosophically, she is a communist.
There are no communist nations in Western Europe.

company and corporate names In general, follow the usage of the company itself. But do not indulge a company in distortions and peculiarities of spelling and punctuation unless the second part of the name is a proper name itself. *Pepisco* (not PepsiCo); *Teleprompter Corp.*

But: *BankAmerica Corp., SmithKline Corp.*

Note, however, that names of products, as opposed to names of companies, must follow the trademarked usage of the manufacturer: *TelePrompTer, TriStar, Jell-O, Band-Aid.*

compared to, contrasted with Use *compared to* to demonstrate similarities. Use *contrasted with* to demonstrate differences.

compressor Not *compresser.*

comprise, compose This jingle may help us remember:
The whole comprises the parts;
The parts are comprised in the whole;
The whole is composed of its parts;
The parts compose the whole.

comptroller, controller *Comptroller* is the preferred word for government financial officers. *Controller* usually applies to financial officers of businesses and to anyone who controls something: *a traffic controller.*

concede See **admit.**

conclave All conclaves are secret. *Secret conclave* is redundant.

confidant, confidante They apply to male and female respectively.

confide To *confide* is to tell or talk about as a secret, to tell confidentially. If a news source confides something to a reporter, it presumably should not appear in the paper. Use another verb.

congregation A convenient collective term that may be applied to churches, synagogues, temples or their memberships.

connote, denote *Connote* means to suggest something beyond the explicit meaning of a word. *Denote* means to be explicit about the meaning.

For some the word war *connotes* glory, for others it *connotes* death.

The word war *denotes* open armed conflict between nations.

consensus *General consensus* is redundant. Note spelling.

Constitution Capitalize when referring to the U.S. Constitution. The Times also capitalizes when referring to the California Constitution, and papers in other states may follow similar procedure.

consulate Capitalize as part of a proper name. Lowercase as a general term: *the British Consulate, the consulate.*

consumer price index Lowercase.

the Continent Capitalize the informal reference to Europe.

continental Capitalize historic references or when part of a proper name: *the Continental Congress, the Continental Army.* Lowercase other usages: *continental breakfast.*

contractions In general, use them only in quoted material or in casual writing: *it's, can't, wouldn't.*

Avoid such forced usages as *it'll* or *would've.*

contrasted with See **compared to.**

controversial issue A redundancy. All issues are controversial.

contusions *Bruises* is a better, briefer word.

convince, persuade A person may be *convinced of* something or *that* he should not do something; but never *to* do something. On the other hand, he may be *persuaded of* something, *that* he should do something or *to* do something.

cooperate, coordinate But: *co-op.*

Copy Editing Symbols

I. Newspaper editing symbols and conventions differ slightly from those used by book publishers.

II. Most of these symbols are standard on the copy desks of most American newspapers. The Los Angeles Times' style differs little if at all.

Abbreviate:　　　We are going on September 27.

Apostrophe:　　　Dont tread on me.

Capitalize:　　　We went to los angeles.
(In book publishing, a double underline indicates small caps rather than full caps; a triple underline is used for full caps.)

Center line:　　　　　　　　　The Weather ⊏

Colon:　　　　　Two vital issues peace and prosperity.

Comma:　　　　He is a tough skillful wary fighter.

Dash:　　　　　One thing war can prevent his election.
(In book publishing, the dash, which is one em space long, is usually marked —.)

Delete:　　　　She trippped at the side door.

End of story:　　# (In book publishing, this often means to leave a line space.)

Hyphenate:　　　She cited the military industrial complex.

Insert:　　　　He wore a bandana.

Italicize:　　　He engineered a coup d'etat. (Ital)
(In book publishing, the words to be italicized are usually underlined.)

Join:　　　　　She wo re her overcoat to day.

Link lines:　　　We are going
　　　　　　　　to Los Angeles.

Lowercase:　　　Some believed him to be a God.

More to come:　　⏤ₘ more ⏤ₘ

New paragraph:　⌊He then announced . . . (or ¶)

Numeral:　　　　She got twenty-one votes.

Period:　　　　Her 21 votes were more than enough⊗

Quotation marks:　He called himself a rogue and peasant slave.

Semicolon:	Armed men poured into the streets the city was a shambles.
Separate:	She lived on the town's main street.
Set bold capitals:	See dialect.
Set bold capitals and lowercase:	See concede.
Spell out:	There were 2 cars in front of the bldg.
Spelling is correct:	He identified himself as Jon Smith.
Transpose:	Powerfiul nations always are in conflict.

copyright sign   Use at end or beginning of copyrighted stories, usually in six-point bold.

co-respondent   In a divorce case. Not to be confused with *correspondent*. Note hyphen.

corporate names   See **company and corporate names.**

corpus delicti   Not the body of a victim but the evidence necessary to establish that any crime has been committed. Italicize.

Cortes   The Spanish legislative body. Capitalize.

Cosa Nostra   A casual reference to the Mafia, it should be used only in quotations.

councilman, councilwoman   Except preceding a proper name.

councilor, counselor   A *councilor* is a member of a council. A *counselor* is one who gives advice.

counter-   In general no hyphen: *counteract, counterspy, countercharge, counterattack, counterirritant, counterproposal.*

countertop   One word.

County Jail   The Los Angeles County jail system may be referred to as *L.A. County Jail* or *County Jail*. Subdivisions also should be capitalized: *Biscailuz Center, Sybil Brand Institute for Women.*

In other jurisdictions, usages may vary.

coup A French word meaning a sudden blow, it may be used as a brief form of *coup d'etat* (the sudden, forcible overthrow of a government).

The word *coup* by itself need not be italicized, but all longer forms should:

coup d'etat, coup de foudre (something that strikes like a thunderbolt), *coup de grace* (a fatal or finishing stroke), *coup de main* (a surprise move in warfare), *coup de maitre* (a stroke of genius), *coup de theatre* (an action for or with sensational effect), *coup d'oeil* (a quick glance or survey)

couple Generally plural in reference to people, but not always:

The couple were married on Saturday at their local church.
Each couple was asked to donate a salad or an entree.

Courtesy Titles and Sex References

I. Courtesy titles

    A. In general refer to women on first reference by first name, middle initial if she uses it, and last name, just as we do men. On second reference, use last name only, with the exceptions noted below. In instances in which the first name does not adequately indicate an individual's sex, try to include pronoun references like *she* and *her*.

    B. The use of *Mr.*, *Mrs.*, *Miss* or *Ms.* is, of course, acceptable in quoted material.

    C. In obituaries, the feminine titles should be used on second reference.

    D. Avoid use of foreign equivalents such as *Mme.* or *Senora*, *Mlle.* or *Senorita*, except when they are used for special effect or in quoted material. *Mmes.* may be used in society columns as an acceptable plural for Mrs. (Society material should of course maintain uniformity of usage within itself.) An exception to the use of foreign titles: *Mme. Chiang Kai-shek.*

E. In society news, features and columns the use of *Mrs.,
Miss* or *Ms.* is acceptable but not mandatory. In entertainment stories, and in the rest of the paper, the last-
name-only rule applies—with the exceptions noted below.

F. A couple may be referred to on first reference by the first
names of each in addition to the surname: *John and Joan
Smith*

If there is any possibility of their relationship being mis-
understood, early reference to their marital ties should be
made:

*Dist. Atty. Joan Smith and her husband, John
John Smith and his wife, Joan Jones
Donny Osmond and his sister, Marie*

G. If a husband and wife, or a man and a woman with the
same last name, are referred to in a story and it is necessary
to distinguish between them, it is best to repeat the first
names on second reference. First names alone may be used
in some features.

H. Exceptions to the last-name-only rule:

1. Historic women may be referred to as *Miss* or *Mrs.* if
it has been customary: *Mrs. Roosevelt, Mrs. Lincoln,
Mme. Curie.*

2. Women whose position or years are deemed to merit it
or whose stature borders on the historic may likewise
be referred to by courtesy titles: *Mrs. (Norman) Chandler, Mrs. Onassis, Miss (Marian) Anderson.*

3. Women who are the victims of crimes of violence or
severe physical accidents should generally be referred to
by courtesy titles. To do otherwise sounds callous and
uncaring.

I. It remains incumbent on the reporter to determine which
courtesy title should be used in a given instance if it is to
be used at all.

Columnists and writers of special features may safely use
the courtesy titles to achieve special stylistic effects.

II. Sex references

   A. Titles

      1. Avoid *chairperson, spokesperson* and similar terms except when groups have specifically informed us that this is their usage. A person may be elected to *chair* a meeting or an organization. The holder of the office should be referred to as *chairman* or *chairwoman,* except as noted above.

      2. The title *congressman* or *congresswoman* is to be avoided in favor of *Rep.* (for representative) or *member of Congress.*

         Assemblywoman and *Councilwoman* are acceptable usages.

      3. When there is no acceptable alternative the official usage should be followed: *Yeoman 1st Class Sally Jackson.*

   B. Avoid stereotyping of careers and jobs or human strengths and weaknesses as if some were peculiarly masculine or feminine. But some traditional forms are so deeply rooted in the language that it is impossible to eradicate them without resorting to awkward and self-conscious substitutes. Make it:

     students, not *college boys* or *co-eds*
     firefighter, not *fireman*
     mail carrier, not *mailman*
     reporter or *journalist,* not *newsman*
     police officer, not *policeman*
     flight attendant, not *steward* or *stewardess*

   Sometimes, of course, there is no satisfactory alternative: *She is a telephone lineman.*

   C. In references to humanity in general, there are some possible alternatives, but writers and editors should be wary of them. The traditional forms often carry desirable nuances of meaning. Think twice before making substitutions like the following:

humanity for *mankind*
average person for *common man*
average citizen for *man in the street*
synthetic or *manufactured* for *man-made*
primitive people for *primitive man*
worker for *workingman*

D. Don't say *woman lawyer* or *male nurse*, for instance, unless it is pertinent.

E. Avoid feminine variants such as *poetess* unless they are so common that a substitution would be awkward. A woman may be described as *aviator, comedian, Jew, poet,* or *sculptor,* but also as an *actress, alumna, Chicana, countess, executrix, masseuse, Rockette, suffragette* or *waitress.*

Do not use *Jewess* or *Negress. Chicana* and *Filipina* are generally accepted.

III. Children should generally be referred to by first names only on second reference, but courtesy titles may be used for deliberate stylistic effect in rare instances.

Children become adults when they reach 18, and their names should be treated accordingly.

IV. To sum up: Treatment of the sexes should be evenhanded and free of assumptions and stereotypes.

Use judgment. Use sensitivity.

courts See **Judicial and Court Titles.**

Cracker Jack, crackerjack Capitalized, a trademarked confection. Lowercased, a slang word that indicates excellence.

crackup One word as noun and adjective.

creole Lowercase when used as a culinary adjective, as in *shrimp creole.* Otherwise capitalize.

crisscross One word.

criterion The plural is *criteria*.

cross- Follow Webster's New World Dictionary in all instances. Hyphenate if the combination is not listed:
cross-country, cross-examine, cross-file

cross fire Two words as a noun. Hyphenate the adjective.

crosshatch(#) Use only in charts and graphs or for special stylistic effect.

the Crown Capitalize when referring to the authority of a monarch as an entity:
properties belonging to the Crown; the Crown colony of Hong Kong

Crown colony Generally applied to Hong Kong, although it would technically embrace such other areas as Pitcairn Island and Belize.

crucial Nothing can be more or less crucial.

Crucifixion Capitalize when referring to a major event in the life of Jesus, but lowercase when used with his name:
the week before the Crucifixion; the crucifixion of Christ.

cruise liner Two words.

cruise missile Lowercase. Two words.

Cub Scout

Cultural Revolution Capitalize the name of the Chinese upheaval of the 1960s. More formally: *Great Proletarian Cultural Revolution.*

currently *Now* is a better, briefer word.

curve ball

customs The organization is the U.S. Customs Service, but the word is lowercased in general references: *going through customs.*

cutthroat   One word.

cyclone   A strong windstorm. *Hurricane* is the preferred term east of the International Date Line; *typhoon* is preferred west of the date line, and *cyclone* or *tornado* is preferred in inland areas.

D

D.A. Use this abbreviation for *district attorney* only in headlines or in direct quotations. Otherwise: *Dist. Atty.* before a name.

Dalai Lama

damsite The site of a dam. One word.

Dar es Salaam No hyphens in the capital of Tanzania. But there are hyphens in *Port-au-Prince,* the capital of Haiti.

dashes Dashes are to separate, hyphens to unite. See under **Punctuation.**

data Like *agenda* and *stamina,* it takes a singular verb: *The data is convincing.*

Datelines

I. In general the names of U.S. cities in datelines should be followed by the abbreviated names of the states in which they are located. Exceptions:

Altanta	*El Paso*	*Minneapolis*
Baltimore	*Fort Worth*	*New Orleans*
Boston	*Honolulu*	*New York*
Chicago	*Houston*	*Oklahoma City*
Cincinnati	*Indianapolis*	*Omaha*
Cleveland	*Las Vegas*	*Philadelphia*
Dallas	*Los Angeles*	*Phoenix*
Denver	*Miami*	*Reno*
Des Moines	*Miami Beach*	*Sacramento*
Detroit	*Milwaukee*	*St. Louis*

Salt Lake City	San Francisco	Tucson
San Antonio	Seattle	Washington
San Diego		

II. In general the names of foreign cities should be followed by the names of the countries in which they are located. Exceptions:

Acapulco	Hanoi	Paris
Amsterdam	Havana	Peking
Athens	Hong Kong	Quebec City
Beirut	Jerusalem	Rio de Janeiro
Bonn	Lisbon	Rome
Brussels	London	Shanghai
Buenos Aires	Macao	Singapore
Cairo	Madrid	Stockholm
Calcutta	Manila	Tehran
Copenhagen	Mexico City	Tel Aviv
East Berlin	Monte Carlo	Tijuana
Ensenada	Montreal	Tokyo
Geneva	Moscow	Toronto
Gibraltar	New Delhi	Vatican City
Guadalajara	Oslo	Vienna
Guatemala City	Ottawa	Warsaw
The Hague	Panama City	West Berlin

III. Some areas that are not independent nations have commonly accepted identities and may be used in datelines:

HAMILTON, Bermuda
BALBOA, Canal Zone
AJACCIO, Corsica
BRISTOL, England
THULE, Greenland
AGANA, Guam
FORT-DE-FRANCE, Martinique
BELFAST, Northern Ireland
GLASGOW, Scotland
PALERMO, Sicily
LHASA, Tibet
CARDIFF, Wales

IV. The names of some small nations may be used in datelines without the name of a city:

Andorra	*Liechtenstein*	*Oman*
Bahrain	*Luxembourg*	*Qatar*
Kuwait	*Maldive Islands*	*San Marino*

V. Use commonly accepted names for divided nations:
East Germany, West Germany
North Korea, South Korea

But use *China* for mainland China and *Taiwan* for the Nationalist regime. Do not use *Red China,* except in direct quotations.

VI. Do not abbreviate names of countries in datelines. Make it:
Canada, Mexico, England, Soviet Union

VII. The names of provinces are not to be included in Canadian datelines. Make it:
HALIFAX, Canada

But make sure that some reference to the province, Nova Scotia in this instance, is included high in the story.

VIII. The city once known as Saigon should appear in datelines thus:
HO CHI MINH CITY, Vietnam

IX. The only time the term *USS* or *HMS* should be used is in datelines:
ON BOARD THE USS NIMITZ—

X. *United Nations* stands alone in datelines.

daylight-saving time   Note hyphen. But: *Eastern Daylight Time, Pacific Standard Time.*

days in leads   Avoid awkward placement of time elements in leads. In general, the time element should follow the verb, but it may precede the verb to avoid an awkward construction. Do not juxtapose a day of the week and a proper noun but separate them with the preposition *on.*

President Carter said Tuesday that he will veto the bill.
President Carter today described his proposal as progressive.
The measure will go to President Carter on Tuesday.

Note that the location of the time element may make a difference to the sense of the story:

President Carter said Tuesday he will veto the bill.
President Carter said he will veto the bill Tuesday.

d.b.a. It means *doing business as*. Avoid it.

DD Doctor of divinity. No comma preceding it when it follows a name.

DDS Doctor of dental surgery. No comma preceding it when it follows a name.

de- In general no hyphen: *deactivate, debrief, decentralize, declassify, decode, dehydrate, detoxify.*
Some exceptions: *de-emphasis, de-escalate, de-ice*

deaf, deaf-mute The word *deaf-mute* has degrading connotations because of its use in the past. And the word is more often than not misapplied to those who are deaf only. Use, in preference, *deaf, the deaf* or *deaf people*. Needless to say, *deaf-and-dumb* is pejorative and should be avoided.

Death Row

deathtrap

decline, refuse *Decline* implies courtesy in the rejection of a proposal. *Refuse* is more emphatic, even blunt.

deejays Acceptable (as a term for disc jockeys) only in the entertainment pages.

deep-sea, deep-water Adjectives.

deities Capitalize all proper names: *God, Allah, the Father, the Son, the Holy Spirit, the Redeemer, the Son of God, Jehovah, Venus, Thor, Quetzalcoatl, Baal, the Great Spirit.*
Lowercase pronoun references to deity.
Lowercase *gods*.

delusion, allusion, illusion   See **allusion.**

demolish   The use of *totally* is redundant.

demurrer   A challenge to the legal sufficiency of a suit without regard to the truth or falsity of the allegations.

denote   See **connote.**

departments   The names of Cabinet departments may be transposed for the sake of brevity: *State Department.* Do not abbreviate *department* except in headlines.

HEW and *HUD* are acceptable abbreviations, especially in headlines, but others should be avoided. Such usages as *State* and *Justice,* standing by themselves, should be confined to direct quotations.

deposed   This modifier should be used with the first reference to any ousted head of state: *the deposed Emperor Bokassa I; the deposed Shah of Iran; the deposed President Idi Amin; the deposed King Constantine.* Later references may legitimately vary: *the ex-emperor, Bokassa; the former shah, Pahlavi* (assuming his full name has been used previously); *Amin; Constantine.*

References to members of their families should follow a similar formula, using the word *former* or the prefix *ex-* rather than the word *deposed.* This in no way controverts such usages as *Duke of Windsor* or *Princess Soraya,* both of whom formerly were members of royalty but whose titles remain.

the Depression   Capitalize references to the *Great Depression.*

Deputy   Capitalize but do not abbreviate when used as a title or part of a title with a name. The same applies to *Assistant.*

Dergue   The military regime in Ethiopia.

derringer

desalinate, desalination   Not *desalinize, desalinization.*

-designate   Always hyphenate combinations. Lowercase.

destroy   All destruction is total. *Totally destroyed* is redundant.

detective Do not abbreviate, even when it is a title.

devil Lowercase. But capitalize *Satan, Lucifer*.

dexterous Not *dextrous*. But: *ambidextrous*.

Dialect

I. Dialect should be used, in quotations or otherwise, only when it is clearly appropriate to the mood and/or substance of a story.

II. Misspellings and typographical distortions confuse, rather than assist, the reader.

III. This being the case, it is better to rely on choice of words, peculiarities of construction or rhythm of speech to convey the feeling of dialect. It takes a good ear, but it is infinitely preferable to misspellings or distortions.

IV. One way to convey dialect without getting involved in distortions:

He spoke with a marked Southern accent.

V. It should, however, be possible to convey the flavor or sense of dialect by picking up the diction of the person quoted. Characteristic terms like *down the road a piece* or *so who's arguing* are perfectly acceptable if quoted accurately.

VI. Faulty grammar in quotations is a similar problem. Slips that are clearly inadvertent or customary in ordinary speech may be corrected without misgivings. But language should not be corrected to make a longshoreman sound like a college professor.

And surely no one would want to deprive the reader of *I should've stood in bed.*

VII. The use of dialect is a matter of avoiding distortions of grammar, punctuation and spelling. Let the rhythm and the diction of an individual's speech convey the flavor. There remains one good rule:

VIII. When in doubt, don't.

dialogue In a dialogue format The Times sets the names of the speakers in boldface followed by a colon:

> **Sen. Johnson:** And how could you justify this?
> **Williams:** It seemed to me that . . .

In an exchange of this kind, each question-and-answer pair should be separated from the others by a slug. No quotation marks should be used. The same applies to this usage:

Question:
Answer:

Q:
A:

diesel engine

dietitian Not *dietician*.

differ from, differ with To *differ from* means to be unlike: *My policy differs from yours in its emphasis on finance.*
To *differ with* means to disagree with: *I differ with you on the subject of finance.*

different from Almost always to be preferred to *different than*, which is permissible only to avoid an elaborately verbose clause.

dinar The basic monetary unit in Algeria, Bahrain, Iraq, Jordan, Kuwait, Libya, South Yemen, Tunisia and Yugoslavia. It is also a coin valued at one-hundredth of a *rial* in Iran. See also **rial.**

diocese Capitalize as part of a proper name: *the Diocese of Fresno, the Fresno Diocese, the diocese.* The same applies to *archdiocese.*

diphthongs See **ae.**

directions Capitalize directions indicating clearly defined areas: *the South, the North, Southern California, Southern Illinois, Down South, West Texas, Northern Virginia.*
Lowercase otherwise: *traveling east, northern East Germany, southern North Dakota.*

dis- In general, no hyphen: *dismember, disassemble, dissuade.*

disc As in *disc jockey, disc harrow, disc brake* or *disc* meaning record or derivations of these. Otherwise: *disk.*

discomfiting, discomforting To *discomfit* is to disconcert, to confuse, to make uneasy, to frustrate. To *discomfort* is to make uncomfortable.
The use of *discomfort* as a synonym for *discomfit* is archaic.

disinterested, uninterested *Disinterested* means impartial, unbiased. *Uninterested* means lacking in interest—quite different. A *disinterested* reporter writes his story without taking sides. An *uninterested* reporter writes a story that is equally uninteresting.

dissension, dissent *Dissension* generally implies violent disagreement or quarreling. *Dissent* indicates a simple difference of opinion.

district attorney Capitalize and abbreviate before a name: *Dist. Atty. Lewis Hill.* Also: *Deputy Dist. Atty. Lewis Hill.* D.A. is acceptable in headlines.

dive bomber, divebomb Noun and verb.

divorcee Do not use unless the divorced status is relevant to the story. It too often appears in such a way as to equate such a status with immorality. Ask yourself whether you would use *bachelor* or *married woman* in a similar context. Would you identify a man as *divorced* in the same situation?

doctor, Dr. Use *Dr.* only for medical doctors, osteopaths, chiropractors, veterinarians and optometrists, and use only on first reference. In other fields, refer to *having his doctorate* or *getting his Ph.D.*
Note, too, that MD is to be used sparingly. When it is used, it is not preceded by a comma, nor does it take periods.

do's and don'ts

double-dip, double-dipping

double-header

doves, hawks Do not capitalize figurative uses.

down- Words with this prefix generally do not take a hyphen: *downhill, downstate, downtime.*

But: *down-home* (the adjective)

-down Webster's New World Dictionary is our authority, as it is that of the wire services. Some examples:

breakdown, countdown, markdown, meltdown, put-down, run-down, sit-down, splashdown

All verbs are two words.

downcourt

Down East Maine.

downriver Both adjective and adverb.

Down Under Australia or New Zealand.

Dr. See **doctor.**

drag race The noun. *Drag-race* is the verb and the adjective. *Drag racer* is another noun. Also: *dragster.*

drag strip

drop kick The noun. Also: *drop-kicker.* The verb is *drop-kick.*

drunk, drunken *Drunk* is the generally accepted idiomatic usage: *He is a drunk; drunk driving; a drunk driver.*

Drunken may be used for special effect. It is idiomatic to refer to *a drunken sailor.*

dry dock Two words. But note:

Norfolk Shipbuilding & Drydock Corp.
Newport News Shipbuilding & Dry Dock Co.

Dutch oven, Dutch treat, Dutch uncle

Dyak The East Indian tribe. Not *Dayak.*

E

earned-run average The abbreviation *ERA* should not be used outside the sports pages nor if there is any danger of confusion with the equal rights amendment.

earring

earth Generally lowercase, it should be capitalized when it is used to denote the planet: *a comet approaching Earth; between Earth and Mars.*

earthmover

East Capitalize to denote a specific region of the United States: *He came to California from the East.*
Also: *the Far East, the Middle East.*
Lowercase when simply a direction: *He moved east to Kansas.*

East Coast

Easter Capitalize. Also *Easter Day.* (*Easter Sunday* is redundant.) The week before Easter, which includes Good Friday, is called *Holy Week.*
Don't confuse it with *Easter Week,* which is the week after Easter.

Eastern Airlines The incorporation papers still read *air lines,* but the one-word usage is part of the company's public identity.

Eastern Bloc The Soviet satellites of Eastern Europe.

Eastern Europe, East Europe

Eastern Seaboard

Eastern Shore Of Maryland and Virginia.

East Germany

Eastside, Eastsider This is Los Angeles usage only. Most other cities, including New York, make it *East Side*.

easygoing

Ecuador, Ecuadorean Not *Ecuadorian*.

Editor, Managing Editor At The Times such words are titles rather than job descriptions and are capitalized before the names. Lowercase below the rank of executive news editor.

Usages at other newspapers may differ.

effect See **affect, effect.**

either . . . or They require a verb that agrees with the nearer subject:

Either the President or the senators are right.
Either the senators or the President is right.

el, al See **the** and **Arabic names.**

elderly Do not use in reference to people under 70. But it may be used in general references: A *home for the elderly*.

But note that *senior citizen* applies to people over 65, the generally accepted retirement age.

This definition of *elderly* goes beyond that of Webster's New World Dictionary but is an arbitrary decision by The Times in an effort to avoid the use of the term when it is clearly inappropriate.

-elect Lowercase in such compounds as *President-elect*.

Election Day Capitalize when referring to the occasion in the United States.

election returns The Times follows this style:

The vote, with 234 of the state's 6,789 precincts reporting:

Smithers	**23,456**	**40.5% of the vote**
Johnson	**22,222**	**38.4%**
Taylor	**12,222**	**21.1%**

On second reference:

The vote, with 240 precincts reporting:

Smithers	**28,777**	**42.8%**
Johnson	**25,234**	**37.5%**
Taylor	**13,333**	**19.8%**

The final results:

Complete returns showed:

Smithers	**234,567**	**41.3%**
Johnson	**222,222**	**39.1%**
Taylor	**111,111**	**19.6%**

the Elks, an Elk

ellipsis See **Punctuation.**

El Salvador, Salvadoran *San Salvador* is the capital of *El Salvador.* Do not use *Salvadorian* or *Salvadorean.*

embarrass, embarrassment

embassy *The French Embassy, the embassy.*

emcee Not *MC.*

emigrate, out-migrate *Emigrate* refers to the movement from one country to another; *out-migrate* implies movement from one region to another within the same country.

the Empire State New York.

employee Not *employe.*

enact Laws are *enacted,* bills are *passed,* resolutions are *adopted.*

Encyclopaedia Britannica Note spelling.

enforceable But the other adjective is *forcible*.

ensure, insure *Ensure* means to make sure of something. *Insure* means to take out an insurance policy.

equal Nothing can be more or less equal.

Equator Capitalize.

equivalent The adjective is followed by *to*: For some people, hunger is *equivalent to* starvation.

The noun is followed by *of*: For some people, hunger is the *equivalent of* starvation.

the Establishment

esthete Make it *aesthete, aesthetic*.

-eth This Middle English verb ending should be used only with the third person singular: *My cup runneth over; from whence cometh my help.*

Similarly, the archaic ending *-st* or *-est* should be used only with the archaic second person singular pronoun *thou*.

Thou goest; thou hast.

Ethnic Designations

I. Ethnic identification of persons in the news should not be made unless it is relevant.

II. Use *black* rather than *Negro*, except in proper names and direct quotations. *Negress* should appear only in direct quotations.

III. Use *Chicano* as an abbreviated synonym for Mexican-American unless it is established that the individual prefers the latter. A reporter should establish the preference rather than make an assumption. Spanish-surnamed families that have been in California since the days of the dons should in particular not be called *Chicanos* unless they prefer it. The use of the feminine *Chicana* is fully acceptable.

IV. *Latino* is the preferred umbrella term for all Spanish-surnamed groups in the United States. *Hispanic* should be used only to refer to persons of Spanish or Portuguese descent.

V. Omit hyphens in *Latin American* and *French Canadian* but not in other compounds: *Polish-American, Mexican-American*.

VI. In general, use the word *white* to refer to the majority group in our society. *Anglo* should be used as a synonym for *white* in stories that deal exclusively with whites and Chicanos, especially, for example, if the Chicanos involved use the term *Anglos* themselves. In Los Angeles school desegregation stories, use *white, black* and *Chicano*.

VII. Illegal aliens

A. *Illegal aliens* is the briefest and simplest term that can be applied to citizens of foreign countries who have come to this country illegally, with no passport, visa or other document to show that they are entitled to visit, work or live in the United States. It is clearly the most suitable headline usage.

B. There is no reason, however, why *illegal immigrants* or *illegal migrants*, whichever is more appropriate, should not be used as synonyms.

C. The terms *undocumented workers* and *undocumented aliens* are euphemisms and should be used only in specific contexts for specific purposes. They are acceptable in free-lance contributions from authorities who prefer them.

D. Neither *illegal alien* nor *illegal migrant* nor *illegal immigrant* should be applied to an individual unless his residence in the United States has been ruled illegal by the Immigration and Naturalization Service. It is clearly libelous if untrue, and it prejudges the individual.

Do not use *wetback* except in direct quotations.

VIII. Use *Asian* or *Asian-American* in preference to *Oriental* when referring to groups or persons, except in direct quotations or the proper names of organizations.

  IX. The word *Jew* should never be used as an adjective, nor should the word *Jewess* be used at all, except in direct quotations.

  X. Capitalize *Colored* when referring to the South African ethnic group.

Euratom   Acceptable in headlines and second references to the European Atomic Energy Community.

Eurocommunism, Eurocommunist

evangelical   A category of doctrinally conservative Christians. *Evangelicals* make up the membership of some denominations and are numerous in others. An *evangelical* is not the same thing as an *evangelist*.

evangelism   Activity outside the confines of individual church groupings to influence others to the Christian faith.

everyone, every one   *Everyone* means *all people, everybody. Every one* means *each one: Everyone is going to the dance; every one of the tickets was sold.*

ex-   When used in the sense of *out of*, no hyphen: *excommunicate, exegesis, exorbitant, extradite, expropriate, expunge, extort.*

When used in the sense of *former*, hyphenate: *ex-Marine, ex-newspaperman, ex-sailor.*

Do not capitalize with a title: *ex-President Nixon.* And make it *ex-California Gov. Ronald Reagan*, not *California ex-Gov. Ronald Reagan.* (Follow a similar style with *then-Gov. Ronald Reagan.*)

When space permits, the word *former* is preferable to *ex.*

except, accept   See **accept.**

exclusives   Such phrases as "The Times learned today" have a valid and important role in many news stories.

Their use should be limited to cases in which the information is truly exclusive with The Times or is of substantial or compelling importance.

Some news stories may call for a second such attribution.

But to apply such phrases to a routinely developed story is to weaken their value.

None of this is intended to discourage the use of such phrases in the appropriate circumstances or to press for their use when they are unjustified.

exit   Do not use as a verb.

expect, anticipate   See **anticipate.**

Explorer Scout

extra-   Do not hyphenate when used in the sense of *outside of* unless it is followed by a word beginning with *a: extramarital, extraordinary, extra-alimentary, extrasensory.*

Use the hyphen when the prefix means *exceptionally: extra-dry drink, extra-big turnout, extra-long workday.*

F

face lift, face lifting   Two nouns. The verb is *face-lift*.

face to face, face-to-face   Adverb and adjective: *They met face to face; he sought a face-to-face encounter.*

famed, famous   These adjectives are rarely necessary. You don't have to tell people that a famous man is famous. But limited fame is possible.
He is famous among the Dyak tribesmen of New Guinea.

Fannie Mae   The Federal National Mortgage Assn. The colloquialism should appear only in financial pages.

Far East

Farsi   The language of Iran. The Times uses *Persian* except when *Farsi* appears in direct quotations.

farther, further   Use *farther* for physical distance only: *farther down the road; New York is farther from St. Louis than Los Angeles.* Use *further* in all other instances.

fascist   Capitalize the party or its members. Lowercase the philosophy or its adherents.
The Fascists came to power under Benito Mussolini.
The racial views of the Ku Klux Klan are fascist in nature.

fastball

Father   Catholic priests should be referred to on first reference as *Father*. Second references take no honorific.
Father James K. Finnegan, Finnegan
The same applies to priests of the Orthodox churches.
See also **Religious References.**

the Father Capitalize in reference to deity.

faze, phase *Faze* means to disconcert or disturb: *The President was not fazed by the criticism.*

Phase indicates a stage or an aspect; as a verb it means to act out by stages: *a phase of her career; he was phasing out some of his activities.*

FBI The abbreviation is generally acceptable.

F.D.R. The initials are acceptable in quotations or in casual references.

the Fed The Federal Reserve System or the Federal Reserve Board. Use on second reference only and primarily in financial pages.

fewer, less *Fewer* generally refers to distinguishable units: *fewer houses, fewer people.*

But: *less alimony, less money, less trouble*

fiancé, fiancée One is the masculine, the other the feminine.

fiber glass, Fiberglas The general name and trade name.

field goal

fiery

Filipino, Filipina Male and female citizens of the Philippines.

final Nothing can be more or less final.

find, locate Do not use *locate* when *find* will do. To *find* is to discover, to *locate* is to place in position.

fine-tune, fine-tuned, fine-tuning

firebomb Always one word, whether noun, adjective or verb.

firefighter, firefighting One word.

But note that the United Firefighters of Los Angeles is a local of the International Association of Fire Fighters.

first baseman

first-class Hyphenate both adjective and adverb.

First Family, First Lady

firsthand Both adjective and adverb. Also: *at firsthand*.

first names First names should generally be used on second reference for persons under the age of 18 and may be used for others in deliberately informal contexts.

fistfight

flack, flak A *flack* is a press agent. *Flak* is anti-aircraft fire and is used figuratively for clamorous opposition or criticism.

flair, flare A *flair* is a natural talent or sense of style. A *flare* is a sudden bright light, a sudden outburst of emotion or a spreading outward (as of a skirt). The verb is analogous: A *skirt flares*.

flammable Not *inflammable*. But the figurative *inflammatory* is acceptable.

flare up The verb. The noun is *flare-up*. See also **flair**.

flash flood The noun. The verb is *flash-flood*.

flaunt, flout To *flaunt* means to display boldly; to *flout* is to mock, to ignore, to show scorn or contempt for.

Fleet Street A general term for the newspaper district of London.

flier, flyer A *flier* is a thing or person that flies. A *flyer* is a fast bus or train, a small handbill or a reckless gamble in the stock market.

flip-top

floods Flood stories usually tell how high the water is and where it is expected to crest. Such stories should also tell what the flood stage is and how high the water is in relation to it.

floodwater, floodwaters One word.

floor covering Two words.

flout, flaunt See **flaunt**.

fluorescent Not *flourescent*.

flutist Not *flautist*.

fly ball Two words.

flyer See **flier**.

-fold Do not hyphenate: *twofold, tenfold, multifold, hundred-fold*.

following When it means after, say *after*.

Foods

I. Spellings and usages of the names of foods vary substantially. The Times relies, in general, on Webster's New World Dictionary of the American Language. Exceptions are indicated in the following examples.

II. Capitalize: *beef Wellington, Bloody Mary, Dutch oven, oysters Rockefeller, Swiss cheese, Romano, Muenster, Edam, Camembert, Gruyere, Curaçao, Cheddar, Jack, Bourguignon, Parker House rolls* (an exception).

III. Lowercase: *napoleon, french fries, manhattan cocktail, hollandaise, akvavit, tequila, longhorn, savoy cabbage, continental, ricotta, epicurean, mozzarella, brandy*.

IV. One word: *eggnog, jellyroll, seafood, spongecake, shellfish, semisweet, meatballs, fruitcake, watercress, cupcake, cornmeal, cornstarch, oatmeal, ladyfingers, potluck, applesauce, cheesecake, mincemeat, cookbook, deluxe, coffeecake, cornflakes*.

V. Two words: *spring form, fish cake, crab meat, corn bread, sea bass, ginger ale, short ribs, club soda, meat loaf, poppy seed, Parker House* (again, an exception).

VI. Hyphenate: *flip-top*.

VII. Spelling: *avgolemono, bearnaise, borscht* (an exception to Webster's New World Dictionary), *Bourguignon, bulgur, cantaloupe, catsup, charoset, cookie, espresso, fettucine, fillet* (except *filet mignon*), *hors d'oeuvres, kebabs, lasagna, MSG,*

Peking duck, piccata, recipe, restaurateur, ricotta, scaloppine, upside-down cake, vinaigrette, whiskey (except for *Scotch* and *Canadian whisky*).

VIII. Usages:

gourmand, gourmet. There is a difference. A *gourmand* is a hearty eater who enjoys and appreciates good food. A *gourmet* is a connoisseur of food and its preparation. It might be said that a gourmand falls somewhere between a glutton and a gourmet.

hot dog, hotdog. A *hot dog* is a food. A *hotdog* is a showoff. *Hot dog!* is an expression of enthusiasm or delight.

teaspoon. There is no need for a terminal *-ful* on the end of the word. In recipes and elsewhere, use *teaspoons* or *tablespoons*.

IX. See **Italics** for usage with foreign names.

footrace

forbear, forebear   To *forbear* is to desist. A *forebear* is an ancestor.

forbid   Takes the preposition *to*, not *from*.

forcible   But *enforceable*.

fore-   Usually no hyphen: *foregather, forefather, foreshorten, foresee*.

forego, forgo   To *forego* is to precede. To *forgo* is to do without. *Forego* is little used except in such terms as *the foregoing material* or *a foregone conclusion*.

foreign cities   Little-known foreign cities should be located with reference to some familiar city or geographical feature. See **geographical names**.

foreign government departments   The French *Foreign Ministry, the ministry.* But not *the office* for the British *Foreign Office.*

foreign legislative bodies Capitalize both the foreign name and the English equivalent: *the Cortes, the Spanish Parliament; the Knesset, the Israeli Parliament.*

Lowercase *parliament* in the general sense: *The Cortes is Spain's parliament.*

Capitalize individual houses: *the French National Assembly.*

The names of national legislative bodies vary considerably—from Andorra's General Council of the Valleys to Mongolia's People's Great Hural—but many of them are parliaments, national assemblies or congresses. In many cases, the English equivalent is to be preferred: *Parliament* rather than *Folketing,* for instance, in Denmark.

Some examples of the different types:

Parliaments: Australia, Canada, Denmark, Finland, France, West Germany, India, Iran, Italy, Norway and Great Britain

National assemblies: Bulgaria, Cuba, Hungary, Ivory Coast, Jordan, Kenya, South Korea, Malta, Nepal, Tanzania, Thailand, Vietnam

National congresses: Argentina, Bolivia, Brazil, Chile, Dominican Republic, Guatemala and Peru

All such bodies are named in the Political Handbook.

Foreign Names

I. Many foreign name usages are covered under the headings **Arabic Names, Asian Names, Russian Names,** and **Spanish and Portuguese Names.** Here it is intended to note a few other usages that may prove puzzling.

II. European names frequently involve such particles as *da, d', de, della, des, du, la, l', ten, ter, van* and *von.*

In general these particles should be lowercased on first reference and repeated and capitalized on second reference unless the writer or editor knows it is omitted by custom or as a matter of personal preference:

Charles de Gaulle, De Gaulle
Luca della Robbia, Della Robbia
Ludwig van Beethoven, Beethoven

III. Writers and editors should be alert for the occasional double surname:

Valery Giscard d'Estaing, Giscard d'Estaing, Giscard (OK in headlines)

IV. English and American names with particles derived from those on the Continent present individual problems and should be considered individually. Such names should be rendered in accordance with historical usage or individual preference; second references should be capitalized.

Lee De Forest, De Forest
Eva Le Gallienne, Le Gallienne
Martin Van Buren, Van Buren
Eamon de Valera, De Valera
Walter de la Mare, De la Mare
William vanden Heuvel, Vanden Heuvel
J. F. terHorst, TerHorst

Foreign Service

foreign words and phrases   Under no circumstances should a foreign word or phrase be used when the editor does not know what it means.

Foreign words that have become proper names in English do not necessarily have to follow the rules that they might have to if translated. We say, for instance, *the La Brea tar pits* even though *la* means *the* and *brea* means *tar*. And we would refer to *the La Habra City Council, the Los Alamos atomic tests* and *the Los Angeles Zoo.*

And while we would refer to *the Nation editorial,* we would also say *the Al Ahram article.* Likewise, it is idiomatic to refer to *the hoi polloi.*

Italics are used with many foreign words and phrases. See **Italics.**

forgo   See **forego.**

forkball

formulas   Not *formulae.*

fort Spell out when part of the name of a community: *Fort Wayne*. Abbreviate the name of a military base: *Ft. Lewis*. The abbreviation is acceptable in headlines in either case.

the Fourth Estate The press.

fractions Spell out fractions standing by themselves: *two-thirds*. Compounds take numerals: 2½.

fracture See **break**.

free-for-all Both noun and adjective.

freehand

free lance The noun is *free lance* or *free-lancer*. The adjective and the verb are *free-lance*.

freestyle In swimming.

free throw

Free World Use only in quotations or in expressions of opinion.

French Canadian No hyphen.

French Foreign Legion, the legion, a legionnaire

freshwater

Frisbee It's a trade name.

frizz, frizzed To *frizz* means to shape into small, tight curls. To refer to a full, bouffant hair style such as an Afro or to hair that is merely disorderly as *frizzed* is clearly wrong.

from . . . to . . . Beware of letting these prepositions become *from . . . and . . .* or *between . . . to . . . .*

front line The noun. Hyphenate the adjective.

front-runner

full- Hyphenate compound adjectives: *full-dress, full-fledged, full-time.*
But note that the adverb is two words: *He worked full time.*
The same applies to *part-time* and *part time*.

fulsome Disgusting or offensive: *fulsome praise*. Not ample or generous.

fundamentalist Applies to groups that have a literal interpretation of the Bible.

fund raising The noun. *Fund-raiser* is also a noun, and *fund-raising* is the adjective.

fungible A technical and legal financial term that should not appear without a definition. A good word to avoid.

funnel, funneled, funneling

furor Correct in all instances. *Furore* is a Briticism.

further See **farther**.

G

gale Technically a wind ranging from 38 to 45 m.p.h. (34-37 knots).

gallbladder One word.

Gang of Four

gantlet, gauntlet A *gantlet* is an ordeal by flogging. A *gauntlet* is a kind of glove.

gas, gasoline In general, use *gas* for natural gas and *gasoline* for the automotive fuel. But generations of drivers have used *gas* in the latter case, and such a usage as *gas station* is fully acceptable. *Gas* may be used for gasoline after the first reference when there is no likelihood of confusion.

gay Use to refer to activist, politically oriented homosexuals or in names of organizations and quotations. Otherwise, say *homosexual*, in headlines as well as in copy. *Gay bar* is idiomatic.

gender A term of grammar, not a synonym for *sex*.

Gentile, Gentiles

geographical names The Times' primary authority for the spelling of geographical names is this book. If a name is not listed here, refer to Webster's New World Dictionary, then to the National Geographic Atlas of the World. Writers and editors should check obscure foreign names, especially those that are new in the news, with the foreign desk, which may have adopted its own usage. See also **Arabic Names** and **Asian Names**.

German states Their chief executives are called *minister presidents: Minister President Franz-Josef Strauss.*

Gestapo tactics

Ghana, Ghanaian

ghetto, ghettos Originally the *ghetto* was a district in Venice, Italy, where there was a cannon foundry (*gettare* means to cast in metal) and to which the city's Jews were restricted after 1516.

It is now used generically for any urban district to which Jews are restricted or to which any ethnic group restricts itself or is restricted by law, poverty or discrimination.

Very often such a term as *area, district, quarter, section* or *slum* is preferable and more accurate. Many such areas have proper names: *Lower East Side, Chinatown, East Los Angeles, Little Tokyo, Soho, Watts* and *Harlem.*

gibe, jibe To *gibe* is to sneer at or to taunt: *The crowd gibed at his failure.*

To *jibe* is to change directions or to agree: *The yacht jibed at the buoy; their stories didn't jibe.*

GI Bill of Rights

girlfriend

Girl Scout

glamour But: *glamorous, glamorize.*

GM Acceptable for General Motors Corp. on second reference or in headlines.

GNP Gross national product. Use on second reference and in headlines.

goalkeeper, goal line, goal posts, goaltender

God Capitalize when referring to the Supreme Being. Lowercase plural references, also *god-awful, godsend, goddamn* and others. See also **deities.**

Lowercase pronoun references to God.

godchild Also *goddaughter, godfather, godliness, godsend.* Always lowercase.

goddamn Lowercase, one word. See also **Obscenity, Profanity and Vulgarity.**

gods and goddesses Lowercase gods and goddesses of polytheistic religions, but capitalize their proper names. Also lowercase references to false gods: *Success was his god.*

Lowercase pronoun references to deity. See also **deities.**

gold rush Lowercase general references: A *gold rush ensued.* Capitalize references to *the Gold Rush of 1848.*

goodby

good will The noun. Hyphenate the adjective: *a reservoir of good will; a good-will gesture.*

GOP Acceptable on first reference and in headlines for the Grand Old Party.

the Gospels Capitalize references to the first four books of the New Testament or general references to Christian doctrine.

Lowercase casual references: *the gospel truth, a gospel singer.*

Gothic Capitalize references to the specific school of architecture, the literary genre or the ethnic group: *a Gothic cathedral, the Goths.*

Lowercase general references: *a gothic atmosphere.*

gourmand, gourmet The first is a hearty eater, the second a connoisseur of food.

Government Bodies and Agencies

I. The name of a local government agency in a datelined story need not include the name of the city if it is the same as the name in the dateline, except when confusion is possible.

II. But agencies in cities for which The Times does not use datelines should include the name of the city: *Los Angeles City Council, San Diego Police Department.*

III. Some government agencies include such words as *national, federal, city, state* and *county* in their official titles; others do not. Editors and writers should check the Congressional Directory, the California Roster and other references to determine capitalization. The Times does capitalize *County Jail, City Council, County Board of Supervisors,* but it is *state Legislature, state Water Project.*

IV. See also **Capitalization.**

governor   Use *Gov.* before proper names.

governor(s) general   Do not hyphenate or abbreviate. Capitalize before a name on first reference.

grades   A few usages: *the first grade, a first-grader, sixth-grade trip.*

graduate   Either *graduated* or *was graduated* is acceptable.

graffiti, graffito   *Graffiti* is plural, *graffito* is singular.

Grand Canal   There is one in Venice, China, Ireland and Alsace.

gray   Not *grey.* But: *greyhound.*

great-   Hyphenate such compounds as *great-grandfather* and *great-aunt.*

greater   Capitalize when used to denote a city and its immediate environs: *Greater Los Angeles, Greater New York, Greater London.*

the Great Leap Forward

greenbelt   One word.

Green Berets

grisly, grizzled, grizzly   *Grisly* means horrifying or repugnant: *a grisly tale of mass suicide.*
Grizzled means streaked with gray or having gray hair: *a grizzled old man.*
Grizzly also means gray or gray-haired but is best limited to one phrase: *a grizzly bear.*

gross national product Lowercase. The abbreviation GNP may be used on second reference and in headlines.

ground breaking The noun is two words. Hyphenate the adjective: *a ground-breaking ceremony.*

grown-up Both noun and adjective.

guerrilla

guest A noun. Do not use as a verb.

gun battle Two words.

gunfight One word. Also: *gunfighter.*

gunrunner

Gypsy, Gypsies Capitalize the ethnic group. Lowercase casual references: *She was a regular gypsy; he loved the gypsy life.*

H

habeas corpus A legal writ or order to secure the prompt release of someone in custody. It should be defined in a news story. Italicize.

Hades

hairdo, hairdos

hair style, hair stylist

half In general make it *half a mile* rather than *a half-mile*. The same applies to *half an hour*.

half- Follow Webster's New World Dictionary and hyphenate if not listed. Some examples:
halfback, halftrack, half brother, half dollar, half-baked, half-life, half-moon, half-truth

half an hour Preferable to *half-hour*.

half-mast, half-staff Use the former in reference to naval ships or bases. Otherwise: *half-staff*.

halo, halos

handcrafted, handmade, handpicked, handshake, handshaking

handful This collective noun may take either a singular or a plural verb. See also **Agreement of Subject and Verb.**

Hanukkah A Jewish festival commemorating the rededication of the Temple in 165 BC.

harass, harassment

hard-line, hard-liner Adjective and noun.

has-been   Noun and adjective.

Hasidic, Hasidism   Not *Hassidic* unless it is spelled this way in the name of an organization.

Hawaii   Do not abbreviate.

hawks, doves

Headlines

I. This book is not a journalism textbook and cannot be a treatise on the writing of headlines. The Los Angeles Times follows rules that have become generally accepted, and the following items are exceptions or special applications.

II. Many headline usages are set forth under **Abbreviations and Acronyms.** Among the abbreviations acceptable in headlines are:

AF, AFB, AFL-CIO, CIA, FBI, FCC, GM, GOP, L.A., LNG, NAACP, N.Y., OK, PTA, S.F., U.N., VD

Avoid such awkward abbreviations as *CEEED* (Californians for an Environment of Excellence, Full Employment and a Strong Economy Through Development).

III. Some other usages:

A. *Vegas* is acceptable, but not *Frisco* or *Philly.*

B. *D.A.* and *Atty. Gen.* may be used without proper names.

C. Avoid *Russ* if possible; *Soviet* is only a little longer.

D. Place names such as *Fort Wayne* and *Mount Laguna* may be abbreviated: *Ft. Wayne, Mt. Laguna.*

IV. The forms of the verb *to be* are generally to be avoided because they frequently serve merely as padding.

A. It is unnecessary to use *is* in *Youth Is Killed in Crash. Youth Killed in Crash* is more succinct and equally clear.

B. When the present progressive occurs, the auxiliary verb is necessary.

U.S. Food Delayed is straightforward and intelligible.

But *U.S. Food Delayed as Europeans Dying* is awkward. Make it *as Europeans Are Dying* or *as Europeans Die.*

C. The auxiliary verb is necessary after *says* and most other verbs of attribution. For instance:

Carter Says Aid Is Blocked
Aid Blocked, Carter Says
Union Leader Says No Offer Is Acceptable
No Offer Acceptable, Union Leader Says

D. But note that such verbs as *consider* do not require the verb *to be*:

Carter Considers War Unlikely
Damage Considered Slight After Crash
U.S. Food Believed Delayed
War Thought Unlikely
Youth Feared Dead in Air Crash

V. A number of words are regarded as undesirable in headlines and should be avoided:

mom, dad, grandma, tots, kids, cops (except in some feature heads)
bare (in the sense of *disclose*)
eye (as a verb)
nab and *nabbed*
probe (may be used if necessary but *inquiry* is preferable)
set (except in the setting of a date)
solon
held (as an attributive except in court decisions)
meet and *win* (as nouns, except in sports stories)

VI. M.P.H. is acceptable, capitalized with periods.

VII. *Said* is an awkward attributive. Avoid it, along with *Said to Be*.

VIII. *Seen* also is awkward. It is generally acceptable when used in the sense of *foreseen* but should not be used in headlines otherwise.

Right: *War Seen if Tension Continues*
Wrong: *Carter Seen Likely to Resign*

IX. All-capital headlines present special problems:

    A. When the present or past tense of *OK* is used, it should be indicated with an apostrophe: *OK'S, OK'D.*

    B. Apostrophes should also be used to indicate the plurals of abbreviations or single letters:
3 PTA'S URGE MORE D'S, FEWER A'S

    C. Names like McNamara or MacDonald should be rendered as *M'NAMARA* and *M'DONALD.*

  X. Numerals are generally preferred to spelled-out numbers in headlines.

head-on Hyphenate both adjective and adverb: *a head-on collision; they collided head-on.*

heaven Lowercase.

heavy-handed The adjective.

heavy snow Technically, heavy snow involves the falling of four or more inches of snow in 12 hours or six or more inches in 24 hours.

height If a height consists of one figure less than 10, it should be spelled out: *a man six feet tall; a carving 15 inches high.*

But if the height consists of two or more elements, or if a decimal or fraction is used, it should be rendered in numerals: *a man 5 feet, 10 inches tall; a statue 5½ feet high.*

Hyphenate adjectival forms before nouns: *a 5-foot, 6-inch man; a 5-foot-3 woman; a 6-6 Laker center* (in sports pages only).

hell, hellfire Lowercase.

Her Majesty, His Majesty

heroic, heroics The former means brave or courageous. *Heroics* are pretentious or extravagant exhibitions of such courage.

hesitancy Not *hesitance*.

high court Lowercase as synonym for Supreme Court and otherwise.

highhanded

High Holy Days *Rosh Hashanah* and *Yom Kippur*. Other Jewish holidays: *Hanukkah, Passover, Purim, Shavuot* and *Succot*.

high octane It does not add to the danger, the drama or the intensity of a gasoline fire if the fuel involved is high-octane. It is merely a fact. See also **volatile.**

high-rise Noun and adjective.

high-risk Adjective.

the High Sierra, the Sierra

high-stick, high-sticked, high-sticking

highways *U.S. 101, Interstate 15, California 74, County 26-A.* On second reference in Times stories, may be referred to simply by number or in the case of California, thus: *State 74.* Newspapers in other states may follow similar practices.

high wind Technically a wind is regarded as high when it reaches a speed of 39 m.p.h. or more.

the Hill Casual reference to Capitol Hill.

Hispanic Avoid except in reference to people of Spanish or Portuguese descent.

historic, historical *Historic* means important or outstanding in history. *Historical* means simply occurring in history.
a historic moment; a historical fact

historical periods and events *The Bronze Age, the Dark Ages, the Space Age, the Defenestration of Prague, the Great Depression (the Depression), Prohibition, the Exodus* (of the Israelites), *the Diet of Worms, the Siege of Lucknow, the Gettysburg Address, the Victorian Era, the Boston Massacre, the Holocaust* (the persecution of the Jews during World War II).

Capitalize *century* when used with a number to denote a specific era: *the 17th Century.*

HMS Her (or His) Majesty's Ship. Use only in datelines or in direct quotations.

hoard, horde A *hoard* is a stored-away supply of goods or money. A *horde* is a crowd of people.

Ho Chi Minh City The former Saigon.

hoi polloi The people, the masses. In spite of the redundancy, the use of *the* in front of it is accepted.

hole in one

holidays *April Fool's Day, Father's Day, Mother's Day, Valentine's Day, Veterans Day.*
Note apostrophes.

Holy Communion, Holy Eucharist

Holy Father, Holy Ghost, Holy Spirit The Holy Father is the Pope.

holy orders

Holy Scripture(s)

Holy See The headquarters of the Roman Catholic Church in Vatican City. Also Rome as the bishopric (or *see*) over which the Pope presides.

Holy Spirit A more recent term for the Holy Ghost.

Holy Week The week before Easter. Do not confuse with *Easter Week,* which is the week following.

homebound Always one word.

home builders, home building, home-building The first two are nouns, the third is the adjective.

home buyers

home-grown

homemade

homemaker, homemaking

homeowner

hometown

hopefully It means *in a hopeful manner*. Do not use to mean *it is hoped, let us hope* or *I hope*. The recent colloquial usage is acceptable only in direct quotations.
Right: *He entered the race hopefully.*
Wrong: *Hopefully he will win the race.*

horde See **hoard.**

horseplayer

horse racing, horse race

host Use as a noun, not a verb. The same applies to *co-host* and *guest.*

hot dog, hotdog A *hot dog* is a sandwich. A *hotdog* is a showoff. *Hot dog!* is an expression of enthusiasm.

hot line Two words without quotation marks or hyphen. But some groups use it differently in proper names: *Hotline Marketing Associates, Hot-Line Duplicating.*
The adjective is *hot-line: a hot-line call to the Kremlin.*

houseclean, housecleaning One word.

house guest Under no circumstances a verb.

House Majority Leader Or *House Minority Leader*. But: *House Democratic leader, House Republican leader, majority leader, minority leader.*

Hsinhua (Xinhua) The New China News Agency. Use the translation rather than either of the transliterations.

Hula Hoop A trade name.

hurricane, typhoon Use *hurricane* if it arises east of the International Date Line and *typhoon* if it arises west of the date line.

Capitalize *hurricane* in such usage as *Hurricane Connie*. But use *it* and *its* in pronoun references, and do not refer to it as *he* or *she*.

Do not refer to a hurricane by the human name only. Make it *the hurricane* on second reference, rather than *Connie* or *Danny*.

hydro- See dictionary. Some examples: *hydroelectric, hydrotherapy*.

hyper- See dictionary. Some examples: *hyperactive, hypertension*.

I

icebox, icecap, ice pack, ice pick

Idaho Abbreviate to *Ida.* in datelines.

illegal aliens This is the simplest term that can be applied to citizens of foreign countries who have come to this country illegally, with no passport, visa or other document to show that they are entitled to visit, work or live in the United States.

There is no reason, however, why *illegal immigrants* or *illegal migrants*, whichever is more appropriate, should not be used as a synonym.

Do not apply either of these three terms to an individual unless his residence in the United States has been ruled illegal by the Immigration and Naturalization Service.

See also **Ethnic Designations.**

illusion, allusion, delusion See **allusion.**

immigration, in-migration *Immigration* and *emigration* refer to movement from one country to another. *In-migration* and *out-migration* refer to movement between regions within a country.

immolate Use only when the idea of a sacrifice is intended.

impact, impacted Avoid *impact* as a synonym for *effect*: A falling plane has *impact*; a presidential order has *effect*.

Impacted has two uses: *an impacted tooth* and a *federally impacted area*. The latter is an area containing large numbers of federal employees or military personnel.

imply, infer To *imply* is to suggest; to *infer* is to draw a conclusion.

in, at See **at, in.**

in- Do not use a hyphen when *in-* means *not: inaccurate, indefinite.*

In other cases the usage varies: *inbound, indoors, infield, in-depth* (as an adjective), *in-group, in-laws.* See Webster's New World Dictionary.

-in Always hyphenate nouns or adjectives: *break-in, cave-in, sit-in.* Verbs are two words.

in-basket, out-basket

Inc., Ltd., S.A. These abbreviations indicating corporate status should not be preceded by commas.

incidentally Not *incidently.*

include, comprise Use *include* to indicate that only part of the total is given. Use *comprise* to indicate that the list is complete.

The committee included two UCLA graduates.

The committee comprised two UCLA graduates and one USC graduate.

See also **comprise.**

Industry, City of Capitalize.

infeasible Not *unfeasible.*

inflammatory *An inflammatory statement.* But make it *flammable,* rather than *inflammable.*

infra- This prefix generally takes no hyphen: *infrahuman, infrasonic, infrastructure.*

initials A person's middle initial is part of his identity and should be used unless he prefers not to use it himself.

When people or places are referred to by initials and periods only, the initials should not be separated by spaces: *F.D.R., U.S.*

But when a person is referred to by his last name with initials, a space should be inserted between the initials: *T. S. Eliot, A. J. P. Taylor, David K. E. Bruce.*

Reference to people by initials only should be restricted to quotations or deliberate casual usages and to those for whom such reference has become common usage: *L.B.J.*, but not *D.D.E.*, for instance.

innovative   Do not use when all that is meant is *new*.

insignia, insignias   Singular and plural.

insure, ensure   See **ensure.**

inter-   As a rule no hyphen: *intercollegiate, inter-European, intercommunicate, interdisciplinary, interfaith, intermarriage, interracial.*

interface   The scientific term has crept into the social sciences and journalism. The *interface* between economics and politics is the area in which the disciplines overlap and interact. A good word to avoid.

the Interior   It's the *secretary of the Interior,* just as it is the *secretary of the Treasury.* It's also the *Department of the Interior,* as well as the *Interior Department.* Note Capitalization and the use of the article. See also **Capitalization.**

interment, internment   *Interment* means burial. *Internment* is a form of detention and confinement.

interpreter, translator   An *interpreter* orally renders spoken statements made in one language into another, instantaneously, at the site of a meeting. A *translator* renders written material into another language, in writing, at some time after the original writing.

intra-   As a rule no hyphen: *intrastate, intracity, intrauterine.*

Iowa   Do not abbreviate.

Iraq, Iraqis   The *Iraqis* speak an *Iraqi* dialect of Arabic.

Iron Curtain

ironic, ironically, irony   When one speaks ironically, the intended meaning of the words is the direct opposite of what might be expected or considered appropriate. It is ironic when a gunman holds up a police station or when a measure designed to lower taxes results in higher taxes. If someone does something stupid and his wife says, "Very clever," she is speaking ironically. The words are often misused, and editors and writers should be wary of them.

irregardless A non-word. Use *regardless*.

Islam The Muslim religion. The adjective is *Islamic*.

the Islands A casual reference to Hawaii.

issue Controversial issue is redundant. All issues are controversial.

Italics

I. Use italics for foreign words or phrases that do not appear in Webster's New World Dictionary and for such terms marked with a double dagger in that dictionary:

ab initio, à bon marché, abrazo, bis, buon giorno, café au lait, dharma, habeas corpus, hors de combat, coup de grace, hôtel de ville, mañana, qui vive, uhuru, vox populi

II. Use italics for words that are NOT marked with a double dagger in the dictionary when they seem sufficiently unfamiliar to justify them:

cacique, couscous, de facto, quid pro quo, au jus, ad infinitum, ad nauseam, amicus curiae

III. Do not use italics for foreign words in the dictionary that are not marked with a double dagger when they seem to have become assimilated into English:

adagio, aria, ad hoc, cacciatore, concierge, détente, entente, banzai, virtuoso, hors d'oeuvres, pharaoh, tycoon, spaghetti, thug, pianissimo, pas de deux

IV. Use of italics is particularly appropriate for foreign, food, legal, medical and scientific stories. Whenever the term used is obscure, it should be translated, defined or explained:

à bon marché, quisling, Potemkin village

Under no circumstances should a foreign word or phrase be used when the editor does not know what it means.

V. Italics should not be used for proper names unless they are part of an italicized passage.

VI. Italics should also be used for prefatory material or editor's notes. When the prefatory material is a quotation, quotation marks are unnecessary. Such material should be accompanied by a 7½-point boldface line of attribution set flush right on a separate line.

VII. Italic passages should not be enclosed in quotation marks, but such marks may be used to set off direct quotations within italicized material.

VIII. A word used as a word should be italicized:

He used the word *intern* when he meant *inter*.

IX. Italics should also be used for biological classifications of plants, animals, insects and microorganisms. Note in these examples that the genus is capitalized but not the species:

Tyrannosaurus rex, Thea japonica, Aedes aegypti, Staphyloccus aureus

On second reference:

T. rex, T. japonica, A. aegypti, S. aureus

X. Poetry should be set in italics when it is quoted in verse form but merely enclosed in quotation marks when it is run into the body of a sentence or a paragraph. The end of one such run-in line and the beginning of another should be indicated with a virgule (and with a capital letter if appropriate).

XI. Italics should be used in preference to capitalization or boldface as a means of emphasis. In general, however, good writing should supply such emphasis naturally without typographical assistance. But the word *not* may be capitalized for such a purpose in some instances, as in II of this section.

XII. Standard book publishing style is to use italics for titles of books and films, but The Times, like most newspapers and many magazines, does not. See **Arts and Letters.**

itemization   Use dashes in a series of paragraphed items:

He had three alternatives:
—To increase wages.
—To hold the line on wages.
—To try to cut wages.

J

jail Do not use as a synonym for *prison*. A *jail* is a place where people are held awaiting trial or while serving brief sentences. Capitalize when it is linked with the name of the jurisdiction: *L.A. County Jail, County Jail.*

Jap A derogatory term. Do not use.

jeep, Jeep Lowercase when referring to military vehicles. Capitalize when referring to the civilian vehicle so trademarked.

jell, jelled Not *gel* or *gelled* except in chemical contexts.

jersey, Jersey Lowercase the article of clothing. Uppercase the cattle or the island they come from.

Jesus The name of the historical figure is correct in all contexts and therefore to be preferred. Either *Christ* or *Jesus Christ* is an acceptable synonym in direct quotations or in exclusively Christian contexts.

Jew, Jewess The word *Jew* should never be used as an adjective. *Jewess* is generally regarded as patronizing or discriminatory. Avoid it.

Jewish Federation Council No hyphen in the Los Angeles organization.

Jewish Holy Scriptures Although they roughly correspond to the Christian Old Testament, they should not be so referred to in a Jewish context. They are divided into three parts: the Pentateuch (also known as the Law or the Torah), the Prophets, and the Hagiographa. All three parts are sometimes described collectively as the *Torah.*

jibe See **gibe.**

jockstrap

Joint Chiefs of Staff

Jordan River, River Jordan Either is acceptable. *River Jordan* is perhaps preferable in biblical contexts.

judgment Not *judgement.*

Judicial and Court Titles

I. At the top of the structure is the U.S. Supreme Court, which may but need not be called the *high court* on second reference or in headlines. It is presided over by Chief Justice Warren E. Burger, whose full title is chief justice of the United States (not of the Supreme Court). Its other members are associate justices and may be referred to thus:

Justice Byron R. White, Associate Justice Byron R. White, Supreme Court Justice Byron R. White, Supreme Court Associate Justice Byron R. White

II. The same rules apply to the state Supreme Court: *Chief Justice Rose Elizabeth Bird* (which is the way she prefers her name used) is *chief justice of California,* etc.

It should be noted that in New York and some other states the Supreme Court is a trial court comparable to California's Superior Court, rather than the state's appellate body.

III. The full proper names of courts at all levels should be capitalized, and capitalization should be retained when the geographical designation is dropped:

the U.S. Supreme Court, the Supreme Court, state Supreme Court, state Court of Appeal (note singular usage), *Superior Court, U.S. Circuit Court, District Court, Municipal Court*

Courts take Arabic numbers:

U.S. 4th Circuit Court of Appeals

IV. The titles of some judges include the word *court* and others do not.

    A. No court in the title:

        U.S. District Judge A. Andrew Hauk, District Judge A. Andrew Hauk, U.S. Circuit Judge John Doe, Municipal Judge Richard Q. Roe

    B. Court needed in title:

        Juvenile Court Judge John M. Jones, Superior Court Judge William Smith

        Note that California has no juvenile courts as such. They are a division of Superior Court.

V. Los Angeles and the state of California have commissioners and referees in their courts as well as judges:

    Municipal Court Commissioner John O. Smith, Superior Court Referee Richard Q. Roe

    Some courts have commissioners serving as pro tem judges. Refer to them as commissioners.

VI. Note the name of the organization:

    State Bar of California (or *California State Bar*)

    But it is the *Los Angeles County Bar Assn.*

    The same is true in many other states.

jumpshot

junta A group or council that rules a nation immediately after a coup. Often a *military junta.* A junta becomes a government after it has set up an organized structure.

juveniles People under the age of 18 are juveniles. They should generally be referred to on second reference by their first names.

K

the Kaaba The Muslim shrine in Mecca that contains the black stone supposedly given to Moses by the angel Gabriel.

kibbutz The plural is *kibbutzim*. Italicize.

kick off, kickoff Avoid the use of either the verb or the noun as a synonym for *to begin* or *a beginning*.

kidnap, kidnaped, kidnaper, kidnaping

killer See **assassin**.

Kleenex A trade name. It is best to say *paper tissue* if possible. The plural should be *Kleenex tissues*, not *Kleenexes*.

knee-deep, knee-high, knee-jerk All adjectives.

Knesset The Israeli Parliament.

knifepoint

Knights of Pythias, the Knights

knock-down, drag-out Either adjective or noun. Note use of comma.

knockout The noun. The verb is two words.

KO, KOd, KOs, TKO Acceptable in sports pages.

Kon-Tiki

Koran Islam's sacred book.

Korean War

kudos   Credit or praise for an achievement; also fame or glory. The word is singular and takes a singular verb.

Ku Klux Klan, the klan, a klansman   Also: *Kleagle John Jackson.*

Kurile Islands   Not *Kuril.*

L

Labor Party, Laborites No *u* even though it's British.

La Brea tar pits In spite of the redundancies, it is perfectly acceptable to say *the La Brea tar pits*. *La Brea* is indeed Spanish for *the tar*, but in English *La Brea* is a place name and the translation is irrelevant. Therefore: *They visited the La Brea tar pits.*
See also **foreign words and phrases.**

lacerations *Cuts,* or *severe cuts,* is better.

Laetrile Capitalize.

La Guardia The man and the airport.

land mine Two words.

land-use Hyphenate both noun and adjective.

Last Supper Capitalize the biblical event. Use quotation marks with the painting: "The Last Supper."

Latin America Do not hyphenate.

Latino Should generally be used as an umbrella term for all Spanish-surnamed people in the United States. Avoid *Hispanic* except in reference to people of Spanish or Portuguese descent.

Latter-day Saints Note the lowercase d. See also **Mormon Church.**

lawbook

lawbreaker, lawbreaking

lawman A law enforcement officer, not an attorney.

lay, lie *Lay* is transitive, *lie* is intransitive. For instance:

The President will *lay* his cards on the table; he *laid* his cards on the table: he has *laid* his cards on the table; he has been *laying* his cards on the table.

The lifeguard *lies* on the beach all day; he *lay* on the beach all day; he has *lain* on the beach all day; he is *lying* on the beach.

L.B.J. Use initials with periods only in quotation or for casual effect. But it's *the LBJ Ranch*.

Leatherneck Capitalize the nickname for a Marine.

leaves, is survived by A person *leaves* an estate but is *survived* by a wife or a husband.

lectern, podium, rostrum, pulpit A speaker stands *at* or *behind* a lectern, *on* a podium or rostrum and *in* a pulpit.

leery Not *leary*.

left, right Lowercase except as part of the name of a political group or a clearly defined political body: *the New Left*.

The same applies to *leftist, left-wing, left of center*.

left-center field

left field, left fielder, left-field fence

left-handed, left-hander

leftover Both noun and adjective are one word.

left-winger

legionnaire's disease Lowercase.

legislative titles California members of the U.S. House of Representatives and members of the California Legislature should be identified by their party and the community they listed as their residence in their sworn affidavits. It is the responsibility of the reporter to ascertain the correct community.

Rep. Charles H. Wilson (D-Hawthorne)
state Sen. John A. Nejedly (R-Walnut Creek)
Assemblywoman Teresa Hughes (D-Los Angeles)

Styles may differ in other states and on other newspapers.

lensman Avoid as a synonym for photographer.

lesbian Lowercase except in the names of organizations.

less, fewer See **fewer.**

Liberty ship An exception to Webster's New World Dictionary.

lie See **lay.**

lifeguard

life style Two words.

light plane Two words.

likable Not *likeable.*

like, as if, as though Use *like* to compare pronouns and nouns. Use *as if* and *as though* to connect clauses:
He ran like a deer.
He ran as if (or *as though*) *a monster were chasing him.*

like- Hyphenate when it means similar: *like-minded, like-natured.*

-like Hyphenate only when preceded by *ll*: *shell-like.* Do not coin compounds.

likely Use primarily as an adjective: *a likely candidate.* It does have an adverbial use as a synonym for *probably*, but this should be avoided unless it is accompanied by *very.*
Do not, for instance, write, *He will likely attend the convention.* But it is acceptable to say, *He will very likely attend the convention.*

linage, lineage The first is the advertising term. The second has to do with ancestry.

linebacker

liquefy, liquefaction Not *liquify, liquification.*

liquidate Avoid as a synonym for *kill* except in direct quotations or when deliberate callous effect is desired.

literally   Means *to the letter, exactly as stated*. Often misused for *figuratively*, which is the exact opposite.

It is correct to say, *He is a bear of a man*, but incorrect to say, *He is literally a bear of a man*.

Little League, Little Leaguer

LL.D.   Note the capitalization and punctuation.

LNG   This abbreviation for *liquefied natural gas* is acceptable in headlines and on second reference. Often *gas* can safely be used in such instances.

-load   *Carload, armload, planeload, truckload, workload*. But don't coin compounds.

local   *Local 18 of the International Brotherhood of Electrical Workers, Local 18, the local*. See also **unions.**

local government institutions   The name of a local government agency in a datelined story need not include the name of the city if it is the same as the name in the dateline, except when confusion is likely to occur.

But names of agencies in cities for which The Times does not use datelines should include the name of the city: *Los Angeles City Council, San Diego Police Department*.

Some agencies include the words *city, state* or *county* in their titles; others do not. Check the California Roster and other references to determine capitalization. The Times capitalizes *County Jail, City Council, County Board of Supervisors*, but it is *state Legislature, state Water Project*.

See also **Capitalization.**

locate   See **find.**

logrolling   One word.

lone   It is redundant to say *a lone gunman. Lone* might be used to accentuate his isolation if he took on an entire SWAT team, but *lone* is clearly out of place if all he did was hold up a liquor store or rob a cabdriver.

-long Usually no hyphen: *daylong, hourlong, weeklong, monthlong, yearlong.*

But use the hyphen when the first part of the word has more than one syllable: *century-long, decade-long, minute-long.*

long-distance Always hyphenate in reference to telephone calls: *a long-distance call; he called long-distance.*

Long Island Do not use in datelines but try to mention it high in a story originating there.

longstanding The adjective. But: *a friend of long standing.*

long term, long-term The latter is the adjective.

long time, longtime The latter is the adjective.

long-winded, long-windedness

look-alike Both noun and adjective.

the Loop In Chicago.

the Lord's Supper

Los Angeles Basin

lot As a collective noun it may take either a singular or a plural verb:
A lot of men were on the picket line.
A lot of soup was left in the pot.

the Lower 48 Alaskan term for the rest of the mainland United States.

the lower house Also: *the upper house.*

lukewarm One word.

-ly Adverbs ending in *-ly* are not connected by a hyphen to the adjectives they modify: *highly improbable.*

M

Mace Also *Chemical Mace*. The preferable generic term is *tear gas spray*. It is permissible, when appropriate, to use *Mace* as a verb.

machine gun, machine-gunned The noun is two words. The verb and the adjective take a hyphen:

He carried a machine gun; they machine-gunned the village; a machine-gun nest; machine-gun fire.

Madagascar The present name of the former Malagasy Republic and the former French colony of Madagascar, *Madagascar* is also the name of the main island of the nation. The residents of the nation are the *Malagasy* people, and the adjective is *Malagasy*.

Mafia, Mafioso *Mafia* is the name of the group, *Mafiosi* that of its members. *Cosa Nostra* is a nickname for the group but should be used only in direct quotations. One member is a *Mafioso*.

magazine names Capitalize the word *magazine* only if it is part of the name of the publication: *Harper's Magazine; Time magazine*

The article *the* need not be capitalized even when it is the first word in the name: *the New Yorker, the New Republic*.

Do not use quotation marks around the names of magazines except when necessary for clarity in headlines.

Magna Charta Note the *h* in *Charta*.

Maine Abbreviate in datelines and following names of cities: *Bangor, Me.*

majority, plurality As used of elections, *majority* means more than half, *plurality* the largest total among three or more.

-maker Words ending in this suffix are usually two words. But: *troublemaker.*

makeup Both noun and adjective. The verb is two words.

Malagasy See **Madagascar.**

man, mankind Either may be used to refer to the entire human race: *the family of man, the story of mankind.*

manager, general manager Capitalize as titles before names.

manhattan cocktail Lowercase.

man-hours

man-made Hyphenate.

mannequins, manikins *Mannequins* are figures constructed for the exhibition of fashions. *Manikins* is an old-fashioned word for little people.

man to man, man-to-man The adverb and the adjective.

marathon Traditionally and most correctly a footrace of 26 miles, 385 yards. Other footraces over long distances should be called *distance races* or *five-mile runs*, for instance.

Another acceptable use of *marathon* is in reference to endurance or distance contests other than footraces: *dance marathon, marathon bargaining session, marathon swim.* In these cases the distance is irrelevant.

marijuana See **pot.**

Marines Capitalize when referring to U.S. forces: *the Marines, the Marine Corps, a Marine landing, a Marine.*

Maritime Provinces Of Canada. Also: *the Maritimes.*

the Mark Taper Forum, the Taper Of the Music Center in Los Angeles.

Marseilles Note the final *s*.

marshal, Marshall *Marshal* is both noun and verb: *parade marshal, to marshal the force, Field Marshal Bernard L. Montgomery*.

Marshall is the most common spelling of the proper name: *Chief Justice John Marshall, Thurgood Marshall*.

Mass Capitalize. But lowercase modifying adjectives, as in *high Mass, low Mass* or *requiem Mass*. The *Mass of the Resurrection* is another name for a requiem Mass. Mass may be *celebrated, said* or *sung*, but *celebrated* is always acceptable.

maxi- Usually used to coin words for temporary use, it should take a hyphen in such cases. Standing alone, it is an article of women's apparel: *a maxi. Maxiskirt* is redundant.

mayors All mayors, including the mayor of Los Angeles, should be identified in first reference by their full names or their preferred nicknames: *Mayor Tom Bradley of Los Angeles, Mayor Edward I. Koch of New York*.

Mcf Thousands of cubic feet. Avoid except on second reference in technical contexts.

225,000 cubic feet is preferable to *225 Mcf*.

MD In general, place *Dr.* before the name rather than *MD* after it. See also **Academic Usages.**

Medal of Honor The name of the highest U.S. military decoration does not take the word *Congressional* before it.

Medicaid, Medi-Cal, Medicare

medium, media One kind of *medium* is a medium of communication, such as radio, television or the press. Its plural is *media*, which should not be used in singular constructions.

All other kinds of *medium* form a plural by adding *-s*.

meltdown

memorandum, memoranda Note plural usage.

menswear

Mercedes-Benz Hyphenate.

METRIC CONVERSION CHART

INTO METRIC			OUT OF METRIC		
If You Know	Multiply By	To Get	If You Know	Multiply By	To Get
LENGTH			**LENGTH**		
inches	2.54	centimeters	millimeters	0.04	inches
feet	30	centimeters	centimeters	0.4	inches
yards	0.91	meters	meters	3.3	feet
miles	1.6	kilometers	kilometers	0.62	miles
AREA			**AREA**		
sq. inches	6.5	sq. centimeters	sq. centimeters	0.16	sq. inches
sq. feet	0.09	sq. meters	sq. meters	1.2	sq. yards
sq. yards	0.8	sq. meters	sq. kilometers	0.4	sq. miles
sq. miles	2.6	sq. kilometers	hectares	2.47	acres
acres	0.4	hectares			
MASS (Weight)			**MASS (Weight)**		
ounces	28	grams	grams	0.035	ounces
pounds	0.45	kilograms	kilograms	2.2	pounds
short ton	0.9	metric ton	metric tons	1.1	short tons
VOLUME			**VOLUME**		
teaspoons	5	milliliters	milliliters	0.03	fluid ounces
tablespoons	15	milliliters	liters	2.1	pints
fluid ounces	30	milliliters	liters	1.06	quarts
cups	0.24	liters	liters	0.26	gallons
pints	0.47	liters	cubic meters	35	cubic feet
quarts	0.95	liters	cubic meters	1.3	cubic yards
gallons	3.8	liters			
cubic feet	0.03	cubic meters			
cubic yards	0.76	cubic meters			
TEMPERATURE			**TEMPERATURE**		
Fahrenheit	Subtract 32 then multiply by 5/9ths	Celsius	Celsius	Multiply by 9/5ths, then add 32	Fahrenheit

metric system   Use metric terms when they are the primary form in which the source of a story has provided information. Each such term should be followed by what is now the more common term in parentheses. In some instances, the parenthetical data might be dropped and a single sentence substituted: A *meter equals 3.3 feet.*

Provide metric equivalents for traditional forms if a metric unit has become generally accepted or widely known or is particularly relevant.

The preceding conversion table is not an indication that every traditional figure must be followed by its metric equivalent or vice versa, but an aid when such conversion is desirable.

Mexican-American   Note hyphen. The word *Chicano* is generally preferable as a synonym. See also **Ethnic Designations.**

micro-   In general no hyphen: *microcosm, microorganism, microfilm.*

mid-   Combinations not listed in Webster's New World Dictionary take a hyphen. Also hyphenate numeral combinations: *the mid-'60s, the mid-1960s, temperatures in the mid-80s.*

midcourt   In tennis.

middle-aged   Usually between 45 and 65. But be wary of age labels.

Middle East

middle initials   Use them when a person wants them used. The more common the name, the more important the initial. When in doubt, use it. See also **initials.**

midnight   *Midnight* comes at the end, not the beginning, of the day. Make it clear that you mean *midnight Tuesday* or *midnight tonight.*

m.p.h.   Capitalize this lowercase abbreviation in headlines.

militancy   Not *militance.*

military titles   See **Abbreviations and Acronyms.**

military units   See **Capitalization.**

mini   Follow Webster's New World Dictionary: *minibus, miniskirt, miniseries, minitrack.* But use hyphens with coined or unfamiliar combinations: *mini-crisis, mini-culture, mini-newspaper, mini-restaurant.*

minister president   Use this title for the chief executives of the West German states: *Minister President Franz-Josef Strauss of Bavaria.*

minuscule   Not *miniscule.*

missiles   Like spaceships and aircraft, they take Arabic numerals: *Pershing 4, SS-2, Titan 2, Minuteman 3, Poseidon C-3.*
Note, too, that *cruise missile* is lowercase.

mobile home Two words. A *mobile home* is designed for permanent year-round living and is moved on its own wheels to a site where it is assembled and mounted on pylons or attached to a permanent foundation. Most mobile homes never move from this initial site. They are built in one to four sections.

Mobile homes are not to be confused with *modular homes* or *motor homes*. *Modular homes* do not have wheels of their own and are not intended to be moved from their original site.

Motor homes are a variety of *recreational vehicles*. See also **RVs.**

Mohammedan Use *Muslim* in all cases.

monies A variant plural for *money*. Avoid except in technical or legal contexts.

months Abbreviate: *Jan., Feb., Aug., Sept., Oct., Nov.* and *Dec.*

moot Its primary meaning is *debatable, open to discussion or debate: a moot point.*

A *moot court* is a mock court in which law students argue hypothetical cases.

Moot also means so hypothetical as not to matter.

more, most To say that someone is *one of the more important* figures in his field is not to say very much. If he deserves to be singled out, he is surely *one of the most important* figures. In a similar vein, it is faint praise to call a place *one of the better restaurants.*

more than, over When referring to amounts it is preferable to use *more than* rather than *over*, which refers primarily to physical position. *Over* may, however, be used to refer to age:

The company has more than 200 employees, most of them over 21; many of them work in a shop over the sales rooms.

The same applies to *less than* and *under*. See also **fewer.**

Mormon Church Acceptable for the Church of Jesus Christ of Latter-day Saints.

-most No hyphen: *northernmost, foremost.*

Moslem Make it *Muslim.*

motor coach Two words.

motor home See **RVs.**

mount Spell out in the name of a community: *Mount Airy, N.C.* Abbreviate the name of a mountain: *Mt. Shasta.*

Ms. Use period. See also **Courtesy Titles and Sex References.**

multi- In general no hyphen: *multicolored, multimillionaire, multimillion-dollar.*

Municipal Code The Times capitalizes the Los Angeles document. But lowercase *building codes.*

murderer See **assassin.**

Murrieta, Murrieta Hot Springs Two California communities. But two streets in Los Angeles are *Murietta Drive* and *Murietta Ave.*

musclebound

the Music Center The Los Angeles complex as a whole. Among its components are the Dorothy Chandler Pavilion, the Ahmanson Theater and the Mark Taper Forum.

On second references: *the Pavilion, the Ahmanson, the Taper.*

The Music Center has a number of support groups and other subsidiaries, among them The Amazing Blue Ribbon, Women Fore the Music Center (no connection with the politically oriented Women For), The Founders, the Opera Associates, the Fraternity of Friends and the Center Theatre Group.

Muslim Not *Moslem* or *Mohammedan.*

mustache, mustached, mustachio, mustachioed Not *moustache.*

N

names The Times, and presumably other papers, should use the name of a person in the form that the person prefers as long as that person is clearly identified. We say *Mayor Tom Bradley* and *Chief Justice Rose Elizabeth Bird.*

A person's title should generally precede the name, but a long and unwieldy title may follow the person's name, lowercased. See also **initials** and **middle initials.**

NAACP Acceptable on first reference for the National Association for the Advancement of Colored People, but the full name should be worked into the story at some point.

NASDAQ Use this capitalized abbreviation for the National Association of Securities Dealers Automated Quotations only in financial pages.

national Some agencies include the word *national* in their title, others do not. The Congressional Quarterly should be checked to determine which is the correct usage. It is, for instance, the *National Bureau of Standards* but the *national Environmental Protection Agency.* The same applies to *federal* and similar designations.

See also **citizen.**

National Council of Churches The generally accepted form for the National Council of the Churches of Christ in the U.S.A. Any other form could be misleading.

National Guard, the Guard, National Guardsman, a guardsman Lowercase the armed forces of other nations.

native See **citizen.**

NATO Acceptable on first reference, but North Atlantic Treaty Organization should be worked into the story at some point.

nauseated, nauseous. *Nauseated* applies to the person. Whatever made the person feel *nauseated* is *nauseous:*
She was nauseated by the nauseous odor.

Navy, the Navy, naval Capitalize *Navy* when it means *U.S. Navy,* but lowercase armed forces of other nations except specific names: *the British navy, the Royal Navy.*

naysayers

Nazi For instance: *a Nazi, the Nazi Party, neo-Nazis.*

NCAA National Collegiate Athletic Assn. Acceptable in sports pages but spell out on first reference elsewhere.

near- Hyphenate when used as a prefix: *near-fatal accident, near-tragedy.*

Negro Use only in direct quotations, proper names and specific sociological material. Avoid *Negress.* See also **Ethnic Designations.**

neither, nor Subjects connected by these correlatives are followed by a verb agreeing with the nearest of the subjects.
Neither the reporters nor the editor was responsible.
Neither the editor nor the reporters were responsible.

the Netherlands Omit *the* in datelines but use it in the body of a story. The name should take a singular verb and singular pronouns. *Holland* may be used in casual references. The adjective is *Dutch.*

the New Left

New World

New York City But: *New York state.*

nickel Not *nickle.*

nicknames The first reference to a person's nickname should be parenthetically included in his full name: *Sen. Henry M. (Scoop)*

Jackson. If a first reference is made later in the story, use quotation marks: *Jackson is sometimes called "Scoop" by his friends.* Later references need no quotation marks.

Nicknames such as *Bill, Art, Ted* and *Mike,* which are clearly recognizable versions of longer names, need no parenthetical reference.

Such appellations as *the Brown Bomber* are not true nicknames but merely fanciful appellations. Follow this usage: *Joe Louis acquired the label "the Brown Bomber" early in his career. . . . Today the Brown Bomber is a fixture on the Las Vegas scene.*

Colorful appellations of other kinds should likewise be capitalized but need no quotation marks: *the Golden State, the Windy City, the Old Dominion, Old Glory, Third World, Iron Curtain.*

No. Use the abbreviation only to designate position or rank: *the No. 1 candidate, the No. 3 draft choice.*

An exception: *No. 10 Downing St.* for the official residence of the British prime minister.

Nobel Follow these usages: *Nobel Prize, Nobel Peace Prize, Nobel Prize for medicine, a Nobel Prize-winning novelist.*

Nobility and Royalty

I. This statement is limited to British royalty and nobility because most of the instances with which we deal are British. Usages of other nations can often be extrapolated from the British but they should be checked with the consulate or embassy of the nation involved.

II. Royalty

    A. Only the monarch and the monarch's immediate family are royal. The monarch's descendants need not be royal, need not be members of the nobility and may well be commoners.

    B. Capitalize *King, Queen, Prince* and *Princess* when used with a proper name, either personal or territorial; otherwise lowercase.

Queen Elizabeth II, Queen Elizabeth, the queen, Elizabeth

Prince Charles; the Prince of Wales; Charles, Prince of Wales; Charles the prince

C. The widow of a monarch is called the *Queen Dowager* or, more popularly when appropriate, the *Queen Mother*.

Queen Mother Elizabeth, the Queen Mother

III. The peerage. There are five degrees of peers—dukes, marquesses, earls, viscounts and barons—and most of them are entitled to sit in the House of Lords.

A. Dukes. The full title is an alternate name:

Arthur, Duke of Wellington; the Duke of Wellington; the duke; Wellington

A duke's children take the title of *Lord* or *Lady* before the full name:

Lady Jane Wellesley, Lady Jane
Lord Charles Cavendish, Lord Charles

The wife of a duke is a duchess:

the Duchess of Wellington, the duchess

B. All other peers may be referred to by the full title:

the Marquess of Milford Haven, Milford Haven
the Earl of Harewood, Harewood

C. The title *Lord* may be used on first reference in all instances:

Lord Bath (for *Marquess of Bath*), *Bath*
Lord Alexander (for *Earl Alexander of Tunis*), *Alexander*
Lord Montgomery (for *Viscount Montgomery of Alamein*), *Montgomery*

D. Peers who are well-known in professional fields may be referred to without the title:

Baron (or *Lord*) *Olivier of Brighton, Lord Olivier, Laurence Olivier, Olivier*
Baron (or *Lord*) *Snow, C. P. Snow, Snow*

E. The wife of a peer takes the title *Lady* without a first name: *Lady Bath.*

More rarely the titles *Marchioness, Countess* (*earl* is the British equivalent of count), *Viscountess* or *Baroness* are used with a place name: *the Countess of Cromartie, the countess.*

F. The children of marquesses take the title *Lord* or *Lady* with the first name. The daughters of earls also take the title *Lady*. Some such children take a secondary title of their father's: Viscount Linley is the son of Princess Margaret and the Earl of Snowdon, who also holds the secondary title Viscount Linley.

G. On the death of the holder of a peerage, the oldest son usually inherits it unless it is a "life peerage" only, as is the case with Lord Olivier and Lord Snow. The son of Lord Alexander, however, became the 2nd Earl Alexander of Tunis.

(There are instances in which a woman may and does inherit a peerage.)

H. The archbishops of Canterbury and York and certain other bishops of the Church of England are called *peers spiritual* and sit in the House of Lords.

Their titles are not hereditary, and their wives have no titles. The two archbishops capitalize the title:

the Most Rev. Donald Coggan, Archbishop of Canterbury; the Archbishop of Canterbury; the archbishop; Coggan

I. The Times does not use *the Hon.* before the names of untitled persons, regardless of their connections, except in society stories in which other similar titles are used.

IV. Knights and baronets are not members of the peerage.

A. Both take *Sir* before full name on first reference: *Sir Harold Wilson, Sir Harold* or *Wilson*

B. Do not use a noble title along with a title of authority: one title at a time!

C. Use *Lady* before the last name of the wife of a knight or a baronet: *Lady Astor.*

D. Women who have achieved knighthood in their own right are titled *Dame: Dame Margot Fonteyn, Dame Margot, Fonteyn.*

noisome Not a synonym for *noisy*, it means harmful or foul-smelling.

nolo contendere Say *no contest*. When unavoidable, italicize it.

non- Hyphenate all combinations except the following:
*nonaggression, nonaligned, nonchalance, noncom,
noncombatant, noncommissioned, noncommittal, nonconformist, nondenominational, nondescript, nondrinker, nonentity,
nonfatal, nonfattening, nonfiction, nonintervention, nonobjective, nonpareil, nonpartisan, nonpoisonous, nonpolitical,
nonprofit, nonsense, nonsmoker, nonsupport, nontoxic,
nonverbal, nonviolent, nonwhite.*
This is a marked departure from Webster's New World Dictionary.

none It sometimes means *not one*; at other times it means *not any.* Follow these examples for agreement of verbs:
*None of the students were there.
None of the faculty was there.
None of the cheese was any good.*
See also **Agreement of Subject and Verb.**

no-no

North Capitalize to define a specific area of the United States: *the North and the South; he went north.*

Northern California

nose to nose, nose-to-nose Adverb and adjective.

not all that This and similar expressions are very popular but have no place in well-edited copy outside of direct quotations:
Wrong: *He was not all that excited.*
Right: *He was not very excited.*
Such terms are acceptable only if a basis for comparison is given.

Novocain

NOW The National Organization for Women. Note the preposition. The abbreviation may be used in second references and in headlines.

number   Follow this usage in verb agreement:

A *number of students are coming.*
The number of students is surprising.

See also **Agreement of Subject and Verb.**

Numbers

I. In general spell out whole numbers below 10 and use figures for 10 and above. But:

5 million, 2½ billion, $3.5 million
Use the decimal only in money or in scientific contexts.

II. Use numerals for:

A. Ages, money, dates, scores, temperatures, votes, odds and percentages:

5 years old, $5 bill, 6-3 gridiron victory, 9 below zero, 2-to-1 odds, 4% interest

Note that there is a difference between AGE and DURATION. Numbers expressing duration should be spelled out. A person, a building, a nation or a document may be *5 years old.* But a strike is a *five-week strike.*

B. Decades:

the Roaring '20s, the 1890s, the mid-'60s, the mid-1960s
(Note use of apostrophes.)

C. Decimal units, legislative districts, earthquake magnitudes, military units, aircraft designations, TV channels, chapters of books, academic course numbers, court designations, highways, street addresses, page numbers, political divisions, quantities in recipes, room numbers, acts and scenes in plays (acts Roman, scenes Arabic), size, speeds, spacecraft designations:

8th Congressional District, 4.5 on the Richter scale, 9th Armored Division, squadron of F-86 Sabres, Channel 7, Chapter 4, Physics 201, U.S. 4th Circuit Court of Appeals, Interstate 5, 202 West 1st St., Page 7, 10th Ward, 2nd Precinct, 2 teaspoons of sugar, Room 8, Act II, Scene 1, a size 7 dress, Gemini 7, 9 m.p.h.

III. When dimensions, measurements, weights or proportions consist of TWO OR MORE elements, or when a decimal or a fraction is used, they should be rendered in numerals:

2 by 4; a 2-by-4; a 2x4; 7 feet, 3 inches by 10 feet, 5 inches; 5 feet, 10 inches tall; 6 years and 5 months; 2 pounds, 6 ounces; 3½ yards; six feet tall

IV. When a SINGLE dimension or measurement below 10 is given, it should be spelled out:

six feet tall, eight-pound baby, four inches of snow, under two feet of water, five miles down the road, the two-yard line

V. Use Roman numerals for wars, for acts of plays and to indicate personal sequence for animals and people:

World War II, Native Dancer II, Queen Elizabeth II, Pope John Paul II, Henry Ford II

But the ship is *Queen Elizabeth 2.* Aircraft, missiles, satellites and space vehicles also take Arabic numerals.

Two exceptions to the general rule: *SALT II* and *Super Bowl XIII*

VI. Spell out numbers

A. At the beginning of sentences. An exception:

1848 was a year of revolutions.

B. In informal or casual usages:

A thousand times no!
Thanks a million.
He walked half a mile.

C. In a series if all the figures involved are less than 10; if one or more of the figures is more than 10, use numerals for them all.

The guard involves six soldiers, six sailors and three Marines.
The project involves 25 dams, 8 bridges and 3 rivers.

D. In fractions. But use numerals in compounds:

two-thirds, 5¼

VII. Hyphenate adjectival forms before nouns:

a 5-foot, 6-inch man; a 5-foot-6 woman; the 9-by-12-foot rug; a $3-million building project

(Note, however, that the usage *a 6-6 Laker center* is fully acceptable in sports pages.)

VIII. Follow the usage of the group in names of organizations:

Committee of One Hundred, Big Three, Pac-10, Twentieth Century Limited, 20th Century-Fox

IX. Use forms like the following to avoid a series of zeros:

5 million flood victims, $10-billion boondoggle, 3-million-man army, 2½ million hungry people, $3.5 billion

(Note use of hyphen.)

X. It is preferable to say *The project will cost from $10 million to $15 million* rather than *The project will cost from $10 to $15 million.*

But the latter construction may be used in headlines if necessary and if confusion is unlikely.

XI. Follow the same rules for ordinal numbers as for cardinals:

first, ninth, 11th, 102nd

XII. In headlines numerals are preferred. Do not use numerals and spelled-out numbers in the same headline.

XIII. Do not use *about, approximately* or *-odd* with precise figures.

XIV. Avoid the use of *some* with figures. *About* is preferable.

number sign (#)   Use only in charts and graphs or for special effect.

Numeiri, Jaafar

O

O, oh   Use *O*, capitalized and without punctuation, before a name in a petition or invocation, or in a commonly accepted unit of exclamation:

O God, have mercy upon us.
O George, look over here a minute, please.
O dear me! O hell!

Use *oh*, followed by either an exclamation point or a comma, in all other instances:

Oh, what a mess this is!
There were, oh, so many people at the beach.
Oh!

oasis   The plural is *oases*.

Obscenity, Profanity and Vulgarity

I. The three words are by no means synonymous. Some definitions from the dictionary:

    A. *Obscenity* refers to words or acts "offensive to one's feelings or to prevailing notions of modesty; lewd . . ." Another definition is simply something "disgusting" or "repulsive." ("Lewd" refers to the showing or exciting of "lust or sexual desire, especially in an offensive way.")

    B. *Profanity* refers to the showing of "disrespect or contempt for sacred things; irreverence."

    C. *Vulgarity* is the state of being "vulgar, crude, coarse, unrefined, boorish, indecent or obscene."

II. Clearly there is some overlapping here:

  A. Such phrases as *fuck you* and *motherfucker* are both obscene and vulgar; *goddamn it* and *Jesus Christ!* are profane, and *bullshit* is merely vulgar.

  B. It can roughly be said that phrases with a sexual connotation are considered obscene, those with a religious connotation are considered profane, and those with an excremental connotation are considered vulgar.

III. No words or phrases in these categories are to be used casually, gratuitously or merely for shock effect. There should always be a clearly definable or compelling reason for their use, as in the Watergate transcriptions when the language involved revealed the atmosphere of the President's office at that time. This is, of course, a question of good taste, good judgment and awareness of writers and editors.

  (Perhaps it is worth noting that while obscenity is generally deemed the most objectionable of the three categories, with profanity and vulgarity following in that order, some profane terms are more offensive than some obscenities to people of strong religious sensibilities.)

IV. None of the terms in these categories should go into the paper without the knowledge of either the managing editor, the associate editor, the editor of the editorial page or one of the assistant managing editors.

 V. We should avoid euphemisms except in the rarest of instances. The use of ------- or g - d --- is prudish. So is the use of *bleep* or *bleeping.* In most instances, it is preferable to say *He muttered an obscenity.* The terms themselves might be used when their use by the speaker constitutes the news: President Eisenhower's *goddamn it* at the TelePrompTer. Such use would also be justified when it is so incongruous as to dramatize a conflict as nothing else could: the late Sen. Joe McCarthy calling President Truman *that son of a bitch.*

VI. The use of such terms may also be justified when it is part of an official record, such as court testimony, and when it is a significant part of the news involved.

VII. Under no circumstances should such words be used in head-lines.

VIII. When they are used elsewhere, spell it:

goddamn, one word, lowercase unless it begins a sentence; *son of a bitch,* four words without hyphen unless used as an adjective: *son-of-a-bitching rat race,* and *bullshit,* one word.

IX. None of these guidelines are substitutes for caution, questioning and good judgment.

oceangoing

odd- Hyphenate: *odd-numbered, odd-appearing, odd-eyed.*

oddball

OECD Acceptable only on second reference for Organization for Economic Cooperation and Development. In most instances, *the organization* is preferable.

off Capitalize in headlines.

off- Hyphenate if not listed in Webster's New World Dictionary: *off-color, off-key, off-season, off-track; offhand, offbeat, offload, offset, offside.*

-off Hyphenate if not listed in Webster's New World Dictionary: *face-off, send-off, stop-off, tip-off; takeoff, blastoff, cutoff, kickoff, spinoff.* An exception to the dictionary: *playoff.*

Verbs are always two words.

office Capitalize when part of a formal name: *Office of Personnel Management, the office.*

Lowercase such usages as *the city attorney's office.*

off limits, off-limits *The nightclub is off limits; the off-limits club.*

off-ramp, on-ramp

Ohio Do not abbreviate.

oil In shipping, oil and oil products are normally measured by the ton. For news stories, convert the tonnage figures to barrels. There are 42 gallons to each barrel of oil. The number of barrels per ton varies, depending on the type of oil used. To convert tonnage to barrels, use the following table, which is based on figures supplied by the American Petroleum Institute.

OIL EQUIVALENCY TABLE

Type of Product	Barrels Per Short Ton (2,000 lbs.)	Barrels Per Metric Ton (2,204.6 lbs.)	Barrels Per Long Ton (2,240 lbs.)
crude oil, foreign	6.349	6.998	7.111
crude oil, domestic	6.770	7.463	7.582
gasoline and naphtha	7.721	8.511	8.648
kerosene	7.053	7.775	7.900
distillate fuel oil	6.580	7.253	7.369
residual fuel oil	6.041	6.660	6.766
lubricating oil	6.349	6.998	7.111
lubricating grease	6.665	7.346	7.464
wax	7.134	7.864	7.990
asphalt	5.540	6.106	6.205
coke	4.990	5.500	5.589
road oil	5.900	6.503	6.608
jelly and petrolatum	6.665	7.346	7.464
liquefied pet. gas	10.526	11.603	11.789
Gilsonite	5.515	6.080	6.177

oil field Two words.

OK, OKd, OKing, OKs Never spell it *okay*. Apostrophes should be used in all-capital headlines: *OK'D.*

the Old City Of Jerusalem.

oldster Often regarded as patronizing.

Old Testament

old-time, old-timer Adjective and noun.

Old West

Old World Capitalize both noun and adjective in referring to Europe.

on Do not use *on* before a date or a day of the week unless its absence would result in juxtaposition of a date or a day with a proper noun: *He will talk to Rick Monday on Tuesday.*

once- Hyphenate compounds: *the once-prominent actor.*

one-man, one-vote The adjective.

one-time Hyphenate the adjective.

only Do not use *only* when referring to a number of casualties.

Orient, Oriental Capitalize. But the term *Asian* is to be preferred describing individuals.

Oriental rug

orthopedic

out- Hyphenate if not listed in Webster's New World Dictionary. Examples: *outbid, outclass, outfight, outflank, outlast, outlive, outpost, outpatient, outstrip, outwait.*

-out Hyphenate if not listed in Webster's New World Dictionary. Examples: *bail-out, cop-out, fallout, flameout, hide-out, knockout, pullout, shoot-out, stakeout, turnout, walkout, workout.* Verbs are always two words.

out-migration See **emigration.**

out of bounds, out-of-bounds *He hit the ball out of bounds; an out-of-bounds ball.*

out of court, out-of-court *The case was settled out of court; an out-of-court settlement.*

over- No hyphen: *overabundance, overall, overenthusiastic, over-indulge, oversensitive.*

-over Follow hyphenation style of Webster's New World Dictionary and hyphenate if not listed there. Some examples are: *pushover, takeover, carry-over.*

Verbs are two words: *turn over a new leaf, take over a company, carry over a deduction.*

over, more than See **more than.**

overall Always one word.

overdramatization If a story is exciting, the facts will speak for themselves without the use of words like *lambaste, slash, flay, lash out* or *blast* when the circumstances do not justify them.

P

Page 1, Part II, Part I-A Note use of Roman numeral for *Part I.*

painkiller

pair May be either singular or plural. See **Agreement of Subject and Verb.**

pan- No hyphen when used with a common noun or adjective: *panacea, pandemic.* But: *Pan-American, Pan-Slavic, Pan-Hellenic.*

pandit Capitalize before a name. Sometimes a proper name: *Mme. Pandit.*

Panhandle Capitalize when referring to specific areas of certain states.

pantsuit

panty hose

papal nuncio See **apostolic delegate.**

paperback Do not use as a verb.

paper work Two words.

Papua New Guinea No hyphen.

parallel Capitalize in reference to latitude: *the 17th Parallel.*

parameter A mathematical term unlikely to figure in a news story, and when it does it should be explained. Not the same as *perimeter.*

paratroops, paratroopers The general term is *paratroops*. Individual members are *paratroopers*.

The paratroops landed, and four paratroopers ran up the flag.

parent Do not use as a verb except in titles or direct quotations. But *parenting* is an acceptable noun.

parliament Capitalize when used as the English equivalent of a foreign legislative body: *the Cortes, the Spanish Parliament*.

Lowercase general and plural usages: *Many countries have parliaments; each country has a parliament.*

See also **foreign legislative bodies.**

parliamentarian A person skilled in parliamentary procedure. Do not use to mean a member of a parliament.

part time, part-time The adverb and the adjective.

pass See **adopt** and **enact.**

passer-by, passers-by

passive voice Many sentences and headlines written in the passive voice could and should be recast in the active.

past tenses Past tenses and some other verb forms sometimes present the problem of whether to double the final consonant in their formation. One easy and generally applicable rule is to double a final consonant if the accent falls on the final syllable and if that final syllable contains a single vowel rather than a diphthong.

Thus in the word *prefer*, the accent falls on the *-fer* and that syllable contains the single vowel *e*. Therefore:

preferred, preferring (but *preferable*)

And in the word *offer*, the accent falls on the *off-*. Therefore:

offered, offering

And in the word *appeal*, the accent falls on the *-peal* but that syllable contains the diphthong *ea*. Therefore:

appealed, appealing

There are exceptions but this is a generally workable rule of thumb. Some more examples:

regretted, controlling, committed, rebelling, occurred, proffered, differing, savoring, flavoring, canceled, explained, assailing, repaired, appearing, regained

peacekeeping

Peking The Times has decided to retain this traditional spelling rather than switch to the Pinyin version of the Chinese capital: *Beijing.*

Pentecostalism A religious movement that believes in physical displays of power by the Holy Spirit such as "speaking in tongues" and healing. Examples of Pentecostal groups are the Assemblies of God, the Pentecostal Holiness Church and the International Church of the Foursquare Gospel. Pentecostalism is chiefly to be distinguished from neo-Pentecostalism in that its adherents have formed new denominations while the neo-Pentecostals have remained within their original groups.

See also **Religious References.**

people, persons In general use *people,* regardless of whether the number is large or small: *There were four people at the door; five hundred people attended the meeting.*

Person should be used to refer to a single individual.

A *people* is a national or racial grouping.

Persons may be used for occasional variety or deliberate formality.

people mover

People's Capitalize and use the apostrophe in proper names unless the group omits it: *People's Liberation Army, Peoples Temple.*

percent One word. Use the percent symbol with numerals in or out of quoted material. If the numeral is a decimal only, a zero should precede it:

Ten percent of the committee was on hand; the attendance was only 10%; an increase of 0.7%.

It is preferable to refer to an increase *from 10% to 11%* rather than to an increase *from 10 to 11%*.

See also **Agreement of Subject and Verb.**

percentage point If an interest rate or a similar figure is increased from, let's say, 5% to 6%, the increase is one percentage point, not 1%. If a percentage is desired, it is an increase of 20%. The one percentage point is one-fifth, or 20%, of 5%.

Peripheral Canal

permanent Nothing can be more permanent or less permanent.

Persian Preferable to *Farsi* in reference to the Iranian language.

personnel Always takes plural verbs and plural pronouns.

persuade, convince See **convince.**

phase, faze See **faze.**

Ph.D. Do not separate from a name with a comma: *James Q. Jones Ph.D.*

Philharmonic It's the Los Angeles Philharmonic. Don't add *orchestra.* This is the prevailing usage in most cities and among professionals. But some groups may use the word *orchestra.*

Philippines As a nation, singular: *The Philippines has* . . . . The islands are the *Philippine Islands* or *the Philippines* and take a plural verb. The word *Philippine* is an adjective. *Filipino* and *Filipina* refer to the nation's citizens.

Philly Use only for deliberate casual effect.

phosphorus, phosphorous The first is the noun, the second the adjective: *This mixture contains phosphorus; that one contains phosphorous acid.*

photog Do not use as a synonym for *photographer.*

Pikes Peak

pinch-hit, pinch-hitter

Ping-Pong

Pinyin   This recently adopted method of transliteration of Chinese names should be used in all cases except the following:

—The geographical names of *Canton, Peking, Inner Mongolia* and *Tibet;*

—The *Pearl, Yellow* and *Yangtse* rivers;

—The names of overseas Chinese, including residents of Taiwan and Hong Kong;

—The names of prominent Chinese leaders who died before the institution of the Pinyin method: *Sun Yat-sen, Mao Tse-tung, Chou En-lai;*

—The *New China News Agency.*

See also **Asian Names.**

pitchout

pizazz

place kick, place-kick, place-kicker   A noun, a verb and another noun.

playmaker   A sports page term.

playoff   One word. An exception to Webster's New World Dictionary.

playwright

plurality   See **majority.**

Plurals

I. Most rules for the formation of plurals are well-known and easy to follow. Here are a few of the others, with some examples and exceptions, but Webster's New World Dictionary is the final authority.

II. Words ending in *-is* change *-is* to *-es:*
oases, theses, parentheses

III. Words ending in *-o* add either *-es* or *-s:*
dominoes, echoes, heroes, vetoes

ghettos, radios, Eskimos, memos, provisos, salvos, tobaccos, UFOs, zeros, mementos

IV. Words ending in *-f*:
leaves, shelves, themselves, thieves
cliffs, bluffs, briefs, roofs, proofs, beliefs, dwarfs

V. Latin-root words ending in *-us: alumni.*
Latin-root words ending in *-a: alumnae.*
An exception: *formulas.*
Latin-root words ending in *-um*:
referendums, stadiums
addenda, curricula, media, memoranda, millennia
A pecularity: *Medium* becomes *media* when it refers to means of communication but becomes *mediums* in other cases.

VI. Greek-root words such as *phenomenon* take an *-a: phenomena.* Also: *criterion, criteria.*

VII. Some words are the same in singular and plural:
corps, chassis, deer, buffalo, antelope, fish, moose, sheep, politics, tactics, economics, mathematics

VIII. Words as words add *-s* only: *no ifs, ands or buts.*
An exception: *do's and don'ts.*

IX. Compound words written solid add an *-s: handfuls.*
Separated compounds or hyphenated compounds make the most significant word plural:
adjutants general, aides-de-camp, courts-martial, sons-in-law, attorneys general, secretaries general, presidents-elect, assistant attorneys general, assistant corporation counsels, deputy sheriffs, major generals, passers-by

X. Most proper names add *-s: the Hatfields and McCoys.*
Most ending in *-es* or *-z* add *-es: the Joneses, the Gomezes.*
Most ending in *-y* add *-s: the Kennedys, the two Germanys.*
Exceptions: *the Alleghenies, the Rockies.*

XI. Figures add -*s*:
the 1890s, a squadron of B-52s, a score in the 70s

XII. Single lowercase letters, single uppercase vowels and the uppercase S add '*s*:
your p's and q's, A's, E's, I's, O's, U's, S's
Other uppercase consonants and multiple letters just add -*s*:
three A's and two Bs, the three Rs, the ABCs, a host of VIPs, a collection of IOUs.

plush, posh *Plush* is a fabric with a soft, thick pile. The slang adjective means luxurious, particularly in reference to furniture. *Posh* is a colloquial term, derived from British slang, that means luxurious, fashionable or elegant. A person's home may be *plush* or *posh* or both, but her china and crystal and silver are *posh*, not *plush*.

It is, however, idiomatic to refer to a person's having *a plush job*, in the sense of a soft job, with little work involved.

podium One stands *on* a podium, *behind* or *at* a lectern, *in* a pulpit and *on* a rostrum.

poetry See **verse**.

point-blank Both adjective and adverb.

police A plural noun, taking plural verbs and plural pronouns.

police department Capitalize when referring to all communities in which this is the proper name: *the Los Angeles Police Department, the Police Department, the department.*

If the department has a different name, such as *Division of Police* or *Department of Public Safety*, this should be capitalized.

Abbreviations such as *LAPD* are acceptable only in headlines.

police titles In the Los Angeles Police Department: Chief, Assistant Chief, Deputy Chief, Commander (Cmdr.), Lieutenant (Lt.), Sergeant (Sgt.), Detective (no longer Investigator) and Officer (not Patrolman or Patrolwoman).

These titles vary from city to city, and an effort should be made to get them right.

policyholder, policy-maker, policy-making

Politburo

politics   May be singular or plural: *Politics is a dirty business; the politics of the city are cutthroat.*

pooh-pooh

pom-pom, pompon   The first is artillery, the second a ball or tuft of fabric or feathers.

pontiff   Lowercase.

Pope

pop fly, pop-up   The latter is both noun and adjective.

pore over, pour over   To *pore over* is to study; to *pour over* is to spill or to decant.

Port-au-Prince

Portuguese names   See **Spanish and Portuguese Names.**

posh   See **plush.**

Possessives

I. The basic rules are well-known. Here are a few of the points that often give trouble.

II. Singular common nouns ending in *s* add *'s* unless the next word begins with *s*:
    the hostess's invitation, the hostess' seat, for goodness' sake
    Two exceptional usages: *for appearance' sake, for conscience' sake*

III. Singular proper names ending in *s* use only an apostrophe:
    Achilles' heel, Dickens' novels, Jesus' birth, Kansas' schools, Tennessee Williams' plays, The Times' editorial position, Keats' poems, Ray Charles' voice.
    But: *Gomez's house, Fairfax's estate*

Note that it is correct to write *The Times' reporter* (a possessive) or *the Times reporter* (an adjectival usage) but not *The Times reporter.*

Similarly: *a Times staff writer, The Times' staff writer*

IV. Plural nouns

    A. Plural nouns not ending in *s* add *'s:*
    women's rights, people's republic

    B. Plural nouns ending in *s* add only an apostrophe: *states' rights, the Joneses' house, the Netherlands' canals*
    But in some cases the apostrophe is dropped when the word is primarily descriptive rather than possessive:
    citizens band radio, a teachers college

    C. In the case of proper names, follow the usage of the entity involved:
    Veterans Administration, National Governors' Conference, Childrens Hospital (in Los Angeles), *Peoples Temple, People's Liberation Army*
    Note these usages: *Mother's Day, Father's Day, Veterans Day, April Fools' Day*

 V. Nouns the same in singular and plural:
    the deer's tracks, the two deer's tracks, the corps' strategy

VI. Personal, interrogative and relative pronouns do not take apostrophes:
    ours, hers, its, theirs, whose, yours

post- Hyphenate forms not listed in the dictionary: *postelection, postwar, post-mortem* (both noun and adjective).

Two exceptions: *postgame, postseason*

post card, postal card

post-mortem Hyphenate.

post office Lowercase current U.S. usage but capitalize, for instance, *General Post Office* (in Britain) or *the Post Office* (referring to earlier U.S. usage).

Capitalize: *U.S. Postal Service, the Postal Service*

pound symbol Use the pound symbol with figures for British pounds sterling: *£100.*

pot Acceptable in headlines, in direct quotations or in deliberately casual writing as a synonym for *marijuana.* Do not use quotation marks.

power play

pre- Hyphenate if not listed in Webster's New World Dictionary. Some examples of both usages: *prearrange, precancel, preclude, preconceive, preempt, prefabricate, preflight, prejudge, premarital, prepay, pretrial, pre-dawn, pre-convention, pre-shrunk.* Some exceptions: *pre-election, pre-eminent, pre-establish, pre-exist, pregame, pre-med, pre-medical.*

predominantly Not *predominately.*

preempt

prefixes See separate listings for the following prefixes:

all-, anti-, bi-, by-, co-, counter-, dis-, down-, ex-, extra-, fore-, full-, half-, hydro-, hyper-, in-, inter-, infra-, intra-, like-, maxi-, mini-, micro-, multi-, non-, off-, out-, over-, pan-, post-, pre-, pro-, re-, self-, semi-, sub-, super-, supra-, trans-, ultra-, un-, under-, up-, wide-.

Four general rules used by The Times are sometimes at variance with Webster's New World Dictionary:

Except for *cooperate, coordinate, preempt* and *reelect,* use a hyphen if the prefix ends with a vowel and the word that follows begins with the same vowel.

Use a hyphen if the word that follows is capitalized.

Use a hyphen to join doubled prefixes: *sub-subculture.*

Use a hyphen if the prefix or compound is not listed in the dictionary or in this book.

pregame

preliminary hearing, preliminary injunction A defendant in a criminal case in California, unless he waives the right, receives a *preliminary hearing* after changes have been brought against him in a criminal complaint or a grand jury indictment. After the *preliminary hearing*, a municipal judge determines whether there is sufficient cause to order the defendant to stand trial.

A *preliminary injunction* is issued in a civil case somewhere between a temporary restraining order and a permanent injunction. (An injunction is a court order.)

premier, prime minister The words are synonymous, but good sense and common usage dictate their use in the following way:

Use *premier* for France and related nations.

Use *premier* for the Communist nations of East Europe and Asia.

Use *premier* for the Canadian provinces, the Australian states and the associated British states of the Caribbean: Antigua, Belize, Bermuda, Dominica, St. Kitts-Nevis-Anguilla and St. Vincent.

Use *chancellor* for Austria and West Germany.

Use *prime minister* in all other instances.

preseason

presently, at present *Presently* means *soon*; *at present* means *now*.

presidency Lowercase.

President Capitalize all references to the President of the United States. Lowercase references to all other presidents except when the title is used before the name: *President Carter; the President of the United States; President Ne Win; Ne Win, president of Burma.*

Presidium Capitalize.

Press Secretary Capitalize the title before a name.

presume See **assume.**

pretrial

preventive Not *preventative*.

priests On first reference: *Father John C. Mulcahy*. On second: *Mulcahy*.

prime minister See *premier*.

prime time Two words. Hyphenate the adjective: *a prime-time show*.

principal, principle A person may be the *principal* of a school and there may be a *principal* reason for his success. It may be the *principle* of democratic self-government.

printmaker, printmaking

prior to *Before* is preferable.

prisons The term covers penitentiaries, correctional institutions and reformatories, in which convicted felons are imprisoned. See also **jail**.

pro- Hyphenate combinations to mean *favoring: pro-abortion, pro-British, pro-democracy, pro-environment, pro-liberal, pro-pacifist*.
Do not hyphenate otherwise.

processor Not *processer*.

prodigy, protégé A *prodigy* is a person of unusual and unexpected talent: *a child prodigy*.
A *protégé* is someone guided or aided by another person in his career: *Eisenhower was a protégé of Gen. George C. Marshall*.

profanity See **Obscenity, Profanity and Vulgarity**.

professor, Prof. Use *Prof.* as a title before names. See also **Academic Usages**.

profit sharing The noun. Hyphenate the adjective.

program, programmed, programming An exception to the rule. See **past tenses**.

-proof Make compounds a single word unless they are coinages.

proofreaders' marks Letters or words that are directions to the printer rather than material to be inserted should be circled to avoid confusion.

Capitals:	caps
Capitals and lowercase:	clc
Close up:	⊂
Colon:	:/
Comma:	,/
Dash:	/—/
Delete:	℘
Delete and close up:	℈
Exclamation mark:	/!/
Hyphen:	/=/
Italics:	ital
Lower:	⊔
Lowercase:	l.c.
Make lines even:	//
Move left:	⊏
Move right:	⊐
No paragraph:	run in
Paragraph:	¶
Parentheses:	(/)
Period:	⊙
Question mark:	/?/
Quotation marks:	᪲ ᪲
Raise:	⊓
Roman:	rom
Restore, retain or let stand:	stet
Semicolon:	;/
Something omitted:	out see copy
Space:	#
Transpose:	tr
Three-em dash:	¾m
Upside down, reverse:	9
Wrong size or style of type:	w.f.

prophecy, prophesy   A *prophecy* is a prediction; to *prophesy* is to make a *prophecy*.

propositions   In stories, *Proposition 13*; in headlines, *Prop. 13*.

protector   Not *protecter*.

Protestant, Protestantism   Use capitals when referring to the Christian denominations that resulted from various breaks from the Roman Catholic Church during the Reformation. These include: Anglicans, Baptists, Congregationalists (United Church of Christ), Methodists, Lutherans, Quakers and Presbyterians.

Protestant should not be applied to Christian Scientists, Jehovah's Witnesses, Mormons or members of the Eastern Orthodox Church.

Protestant Episcopal Church   A more formal term for the Episcopal Church.

protester   Not *protestor*.

provinces   Do not use the names of Canadian provinces in datelines. Such names should appear high in a story.

Provisional wing   Of the Irish Republican Army. Also called *Provos*.

publications   Some examples: *the Los Angeles Times (The Times), the New York Times, the Washington Post, the New Yorker, the Reader's Digest, Harper's Magazine, Time magazine, Le Figaro, Al Ahram, Die Welt, Stern, Home magazine, View section.*

Note the lowercase English articles.

See also **Arts and Letters.**

pulpit   A speaker stands *in* a pulpit, *on* a podium or rostrum and *at* or *behind* a lectern.

Punctuation

I.   Punctuation is to clarify. If it confuses, change it or get rid of it.

II. The basic rules are to be found in Webster's New World Dictionary, under the heading "Guide to Punctuation and Mechanics." Some exceptions and special cases are given here, as well as a few usages repeated for the sake of emphasis.

APOSTROPHE

1. Use an apostrophe in forming plurals of single lowercase letters, single uppercase vowels and the uppercase S:

   Mind your p's and q's; A's, E's, I's, O's, U's, S's

2. Do not use an apostrophe in forming plurals of other uppercase consonants and multiple letters:

   Cs, Zs, three A's and two Bs, the three Rs, the ABCs

3. Do not use an apostrophe in forming plurals of numbers or non-nouns:

   the 1890s, a squadron of B-52s, a score in the high 70s, no ifs, ands or buts

   An exception: *a few do's and don'ts*

4. Use an apostrophe in such idiomatic phrases as:

   a week's pay, a stone's throw, for goodness' sake

   But omit it in cases in which the usage is more adjectival than possessive:

   Actors Equity, Teamsters Union, citizens band, childrens hospital

   Note also: *Mother's Day, Veterans Day, Court of St. James's*

5. Use an apostrophe to form plurals of letters and abbreviations in uppercase headlines:

   PTA'S FIRST RULING OK'S
   SCHOOL'S A'S, B'S AND C'S

6. For other uses of the apostrophe see **Possessives.**

COLON

1. Use a colon before a long, formal quotation or statement:

   President Lincoln spoke as follows: "Four score and seven years ago . . . ."

2. In general use a colon to introduce quoted material only when the material consists of more than one sentence. (If the material does consist of a simple sentence, a comma is to be preferred.)

An exception for deliberate emphasis:

He said only two things are certain: "Death and taxes."
He said his country had but one alternative: "War."

3. The first word following a colon should be capitalized if the material constitutes a complete sentence. Otherwise lowercase.

    He made up his mind to do two things: He would go home and he would go to bed.
    He made up his mind to do two things: to go home and to go to bed.

    Note the exception in Rule 2, above.

4. A colon may be used after a main statement when the succeeding statements explain the main one:

    A newspaper reporter has many responsibilities: He must be judicious in taking the word of his sources; he must weigh the merits of conflicting statements, and he must above all be accurate in his account of what has transpired.

5. Use a colon, not a dash, in question-and-answer material or similar dialogue forms.

COMMA

1. Use a comma when it makes sense and when it makes the sentence clearer to the reader.

2. Use commas in compound sentences before the conjunctions *and, but* and *for*:

    The President said goodby to Begin, and Begin flew on to Cairo.

    Do not use a comma when the subject is the same in both parts of the sentence:

    The President said goodby to Begin and returned to Washington.

    Do not use a comma when the sentence or its components are brief:

    He said goodby but the parting was brief.

3. Use commas in a series but not before the conjunction:
   The colors of the flag are red, white and blue.

4. If the items in a series are long and include commas, use the semicolon to separate the items with a comma before the conjunction:
   The dead were identified as Harry B. Wellcome of Los Angeles, a bricklayer; Jane Evans of Anaheim, a stenographer, and William L. Trenholme of Chico, a bartender.

5. Use commas to separate adjectives modifying the same noun if you could substitute the word *and* for the comma:
   He is a tough, skillful, wary fighter.
   But: *He is a dear old man.*

6. Do not use a comma to separate a name on first reference from an accompanying address:
   Harry B. Wellcome of Los Angeles
   But if the address or similar identification is given after a second reference, use the comma:
   Wellcome, of Los Angeles; Trenholme, of USC

7. Use commas to set off nonessential clauses from the rest of a sentence:
   The house, which has three bedrooms and two baths, is for sale.
   The house that he has lived in all his life is for sale.
   Note the *that-which* usage.

8. Use commas to set off a nonessential appositive noun:
   He took his son, Mark. (Mark is his only son.)
   He took his son Mark. (He has or may have other sons.)
   He died in the home of the singer Sally Fiorello.
   He died in the home of a singer, Sally Fiorello.

   In brief: Use commas when the identifying noun could be dispensed with; if the noun is necessary, don't use the comma.

9. Use commas to set off numbers in apposition:

The Dodgers won, 4 to 2, on a ninth-inning home run.
The Dodgers won a 4-2 victory on a ninth-inning home run.

10. Do not use commas before *Sr., Jr., Inc., Ltd., S.A.,* academic degrees or religious designations:

Martin Luther King Sr.,
Timothy Jordan Ph.D.,
Father Daniel Berrigan SJ

DASH

1. The dash separates, the hyphen joins.

2. Use dashes to indicate abrupt changes in thought, continuity and pace:

His attitude was rather casual—to put it mildly—about the job.
The Four Horsemen of the Apocalypse—War, Famine, Death and Pestilence—rode roughshod over Cambodia.

3. Use a dash between the end of a quotation and the name of the author:

". . . shall not perish from the earth."
—Abraham Lincoln

4. Use dashes in a series of paragraphed items:

He had three alternatives:
—To increase wages.
—To hold the line on wages.
—To try to cut wages.

5. Use a colon, rather than a dash, in question-and-answer formats and similar dialogue material.

ELLIPSIS

1. When an ellipsis is used at the end of a sentence, add a fourth point as a period or supply other appropriate punctuation:

"I come to bury Caesar . . . ."
"Great God, I'd rather be a pagan . . . ."

2. When an ellipsis is used at the start of a sentence, capitalize the first word:

". . . *Our fathers brought forth on this continent* . . . ."

EXCLAMATION POINT

Use the exclamation point to express excitement or vehemence. Do not use after mild interjections or mildly exclamatory sentences.

HYPHEN

1. Even the experts are driven to despair. Yet the hyphen can be extremely useful, and there are a few guidelines. Webster's New World Dictionary is The Times' ultimate authority (with a few notable exceptions).

2. Hyphens are joiners and should be used to avoid ambiguity or to form a single idea from two or more words:
   The President will speak to small-business men.
   He re-covered his roof; he recovered his health.
   high-speed lane, large-scale project, half-baked.

3. Compounds that appear in regular order and are easily comprehensible do not need hyphens:
   atomic energy plant, citizens band radio, high school student (an exception to Webster's New World Dictionary), *whistle stop tour, workers compensation laws*

4. Use a hyphen to clarify figurative or improvised terms:
   pay-as-you-go plan; happy-go-lucky; one-man, one-vote ruling; knock-down, drag-out fight; come-as-you-are party

5. When a compound word is used as a noun, it may be one word, more than one word or hyphenated. The only recourse is to Webster's New World; if it isn't listed make it more than one word. For instance:
   moneymaking, firefighting, time saver, cure-all, worldbeater

6. When a compound word is used as an adjective preceding a noun, use hyphens to link all the words in the compound except adverbs ending in *-ly:*

part-time job, run-on sentences, time-saving device, well-known actress, lower-income group, 7-foot-6 giant, $30-million project, multimillion-dollar aid bill, ninth-inning cliffhanger, 54-28 Senate vote, word-of-mouth publicity

But: *partly finished job, poorly constructed sentence*

7. When the same terms follow the noun modified or are used as adverbs, the hyphens are omitted:

   He works part time; he stands 7 feet 6; the Senate voted, 54 to 28; the rumor spread by word of mouth.

8. Use the hyphen to designate dual heritage: *Mexican-American, Italian-American.*

   But not *French Canadian* or *Latin American.* See also **Ethnic Designations.**

9. Do not hyphenate foreign phrases used as modifiers: *ad hoc committee, antebellum mansion.*

10. Titles should be hyphenated only to indicate non-incumbency or combined offices:

    secretary-treasurer, senator-elect, then-President

    But: *secretary general, consul general, adjutant general*

11. Retain hyphens in suspended combinations: *fifth- and sixth-graders.*

12. Some other hyphen usages:
    a. To join a single capital letter to a noun or a verb:
       H-bomb, T-shaped, U-boat, V-necked, X-ray
    b. With figurative expressions using an apostrophe in the first element:
       bull's-eye, cat's-paw, no-man's-land (an exception to Webster's New World Dictionary)
    c. With numerical combinations:
       1½-ton truck, 3-million-man army, $2-billion aid bill

13. A major use of the hyphen is with certain prefixes and suffixes, and many of these usages differ from those in Webster's New World Dictionary. See individual entries for the different prefixes and suffixes.

PARENTHESES AND BRACKETS

1. Parentheses are used by a writer to indicate an interruption or an interpolation in his own copy.

   Brackets are used by an editor to interpolate material (particularly into direct quotations or text material) from some other source.

   But editors may use parentheses to interpolate routine material into news stories.

2. Use parentheses to enclose:

   a. Nicknames on first reference: *O. A. (Bum) Phillips.*

      But do not make it *George Herman (Babe) Ruth,* who is a household word as *Babe Ruth,* and do not parenthesize designations derived from proper names. Do not, for instance, make it *William A. (Bill) Johnson* or *James R. (Jim) Drake.*

   b. Fuller identification:

      "I told (former Budget Director Bert) Lance he was wrong," a friend said.

   c. A political-geographic designation:

      Sen. Alan Cranston (D-Calif.)

   d. Figures or letters in a series within a paragraph:

      He said he was resigning because of (a) ill health, (b) financial problems and (c) his embarrassment over the current City Hall scandal.

   e. A specific location that would otherwise be ambiguous:

      the Albany (N.Y.) City Council, the Portland (Me.) Express

3. The use of the six-point line From Times Wire Services before the lead of a story often makes brackets unnecessary.

4. Periods go outside closing parentheses if the foregoing material is not a complete sentence, inside if it is.

PERIODS

Use periods after initials of personal names: :s

John F. Kennedy, Harry S. Truman (a departure from previous style) *F.D.R.* (no spaces), *T. S. Eliot* (space between initials)

But: *LBJ Ranch*

See also **Abbreviations and Acronyms** and **initials**.

QUESTION MARK

Place question marks inside or outside quotation marks, depending on the context:

"How did you like 'Star Wars'?" he asked.
"Did you read 'Why Are We in Vietnam?' " he asked.

QUOTATION MARKS

1. Do not use quotation marks to enclose routine words or phrases. There is no point in saying, for instance:

   He said it was a "historic" occasion.

2. If a paragraph of quoted material is followed by another paragraph continuing the quotation, do not put close-quote marks at the end of the first one. But do put open-quote marks at the beginning of the second paragraph:

   He said, "Action must be taken to avert total war.
   "Therefore, I am withdrawing our troops."

   But if the quoted material in the first paragraph is not a complete sentence, do use close-quote marks at the end of the first paragraph:

   He said action had to be taken "to avert total war."
   "Therefore, I am withdrawing our troops," he continued.

3. Do not use quotation marks in question-and-answer or similar dialogue formats.

4. Do not use quotation marks with complete texts, condensed texts or extensive textual excerpts.

5. Use quotation marks as indicated under **Arts and Letters** around titles of works of art and the like.

6. Do not use quotation marks around nicknames on first reference.

7. Use quotation marks for misnomers or ironic references:

   His "yacht" was merely a rowboat with an outboard motor.

8. Use quotation marks for a word or words being introduced or defined for the reader, but do not repeat them on second reference:

   A *"détente" is a lessening of tension or hostility among nations. The present détente* . . . .

9. Always use single-quote marks in headlines and place them around potentially confusing terms:

   'New Yorker' Fights Postal Increase (the magazine)

10. Do not use quotation marks around the names of pets, ships, teams, special events or other capitalized appellations, except when confusion could occur.

11. Do not use quotation marks around italicized material unless it is part of an entire italicized passage.

12. Do not use quotes around generally recognized slang expressions.

13. Sequence of punctuation:

    a. Periods and commas always go inside quotation marks, both double and single.

    b. Colons and semicolons go outside quotation marks.

    c. Question marks go inside or outside, depending on whether they apply to the quotation only or the entire sentence.

SEMICOLON

1. Use semicolons to separate a series of items that contain commas, but use a comma following the second-to-last item:

   The committee consists of Thomas J. Hughes of Inglewood, chairman of Afrodynamics Inc.; the Rev. Walter A. Jackson, pastor of St. Ambrose Lutheran Church, La Mirada; Helen O'Keefe of Glendale, treasurer of Sportsmen United Against the High-Powered Rifle, and Capt. Nathan Wong of San Diego, a retired Marine Corps officer.

2. Use semicolons in headlines to separate independent clauses:

Plane Hits Pikes Peak; 50 Feared Dead

3. In appropriate instances in editorials, Op-Ed pages, Opinion pages and other areas of more formal writing, particularly when the column measure is wide, the semicolon may be used to indicate a close connection between the idea in the preceding sentence and that in the sentence following:

The war is almost over. Rebels and loyalists alike are laying down their arms. Peace envoys are scuttling back and forth between the two factions. U.S. aid in millions of dollars awaits only the signing of a treaty.

There is nothing intrinsically wrong with this paragraph, but the sentences would be linked together more clearly if all the periods became semicolons except the last one.

The war is almost over; rebels and loyalists alike are laying down their arms; peace envoys are scuttling back and forth between the two factions; U.S. aid in millions of dollars awaits only the signing of a treaty.

(The first clause here could clearly end with a colon, but that is a matter of taste.)

puns A pun is more than entertainment. It can be used effectively to convey a deeper truth than the mere play on words might indicate. The mere fact of resemblance in sound is not enough to make a pun effective. Do not try to make a pun unless both the meanings in the play on a word are relevant.

Purim A Jewish holiday commemorating the deliverance of the Jews by Esther.

push-up

Pygmy Not *Pigmy*. Capitalize references to African tribal groups. Lowercase references to small creatures: *a pygmy elephant*. Do not use as a synonym for small human beings in general.

Q

Q&A See **dialogue.**

quadraphonic

quadriplegic

quarterfinal

quarter horse

Quebec province

Queen Mother

Quonset hut

quotation marks See **Punctuation.**

quotations When a sentence contains a partial direct quotation, the grammar of the quotation must jibe with that of the remainder of the sentence. If this is impossible—and it can happen —it may be necessary to dispense with the quotation marks and recast the quotation in indirect speech.

For instance: *Haldeman said he had "racked my brain trying to remember what was said."*

Here it is necessary for the possessive *my* to agree with the subject, *Haldeman.* Therefore, recast the sentence in one of the following ways:

Haldeman said he had racked his brain trying to remember what was said.

Haldeman said, "I have racked my brain trying to remember what was said."

quotations, corrections of Faulty grammar in direct quotations is a persistent problem. Slips that are clearly inadvertent or customary in ordinary speech may be corrected without misgivings. But language should not be corrected to make a longshoreman sound like a college professor.

R

rabbi   Capitalize the title before a name on first reference to the head of a Jewish congregation. On second reference, omit the honorific and use the last name only.

race track   Two words.

rack, wrack   The noun *rack* applies to various types of framework, often frames upon which things are stretched, like an instrument of torture.
He was racked with indecision; body all achin' and racked with pain.
These are, of course, verbs, but one might also say: *He was hung upon a rack of self-doubt and uncertainty.*
The noun *wrack* means ruin or destruction, and the most common usage is *wrack and ruin.* The verb *wrack* has roughly the same meaning as *rack,* which is preferred.

racket, racquet   Use *racket* when referring to a game such as tennis or squash, but use a *racquet* to play racquets or racquetball.

rainproof

rangeland   One word.

rank and file   Plural in construction. Hyphenate the adjective.

raze   To *raze* is to *level* in the sense of to *destroy.* It is redundant to write *razed to the ground.*

R&B   Acceptable for *rhythm and blues* only in the entertainment pages.

R&R Acceptable for *rock 'n' roll* only in the entertainment pages. Elsewhere, *R&R* is accepted as a second reference for *rest and recuperation* in the armed forces.

RBIs Acceptable only in the sports pages.

re- Use a hyphen for combinations unlisted in Webster's New World Dictionary. Some exceptions based on the general rules for prefixes: *re-emerge, re-employ, re-enact, re-enlist, re-enter, re-entry, re-establish, re-examine.*

But note: *reelect.*

A case in which sense dictates a hyphen: *re-form* (form again), *reform* (improve). There are a number of others.

ready-made

reborn Do not use as a synonym for *"born-again"* in the religious sense.

rebut, refute See **refute.**

re-creating With a hyphen, this means making anew.

refer, allude To *refer to* is to name; to *allude to* is to refer to indirectly. See also **allude.**

reference works Do not use quotation marks around the names of almanacs, directories, encyclopedias, gazetteers, handbooks, and similar books. Use quotation marks around similar volumes that are the work of clearly specific authors:

Jane's Fighting Ships; Fowler's "Modern English Usage"

refute To *refute* is to destroy by argument, to prove mistaken. Often misused for *rebut,* which means to contradict or argue against.

religious May be used as a lowercase noun to describe cloistered clergy and nuns. Use only when reference is clear.

Religious References

I. Religious beliefs are an important part of the lives of many newspaper readers, and writers and editors should be accurate in this particularly sensitive area.

II. The major Christian groupings are the Roman Catholic, the Protestant and the Eastern Orthodox churches.

III. Herewith a brief rundown on the major bodies in the United States, including the non-Christian.

Unless otherwise indicated, ministers and priests use *the Rev.* before the full name. The Times uses no honorific on second references. The same is true of female members of the clergy. Some Roman Catholic brothers and sisters, who are not members of the clergy, have only one name. In such cases, they retain the title on second references. See also **Courtesy Titles and Sex References.**

THE ANGLICAN COMMUNION

Consists of 22 separate Anglican churches, each of which is independent. Members of the communion include the Church of England and, in the United States, the Protestant Episcopal Church. (See EPISCOPAL CHURCH below.)

Anglicans who stress the sacraments and extensive ritual are sometimes called *Anglo-Catholics* and prefer not to be considered as Protestants.

BAPTIST CHURCHES

The word *church* should not be applied to any Baptist unit except the local church.

The largest Baptist body in the United States is the nationwide Southern Baptist Convention. Other major bodies are the predominantly white American Baptist Churches in the U.S.A. and three predominantly black groups: the National Baptist Convention of America, the National Baptist Convention U.S.A. Inc., and the Progressive National Baptist Convention Inc.

Members of the Baptist clergy are called *ministers*. A minister who heads a congregation is also a *pastor*.

BUDDHISM

There are two major divisions, the Mahayana of northern Asia and the Terevada of southern Asia. Buddhist congregations in the United States tend to be divided along ethnic lines, among them the Korean, the Japanese, the Tibetan and the Vietnamese, and then along sectarian lines within the ethnic group.

Japanese Buddhist congregations are often called churches, but the designation *temple* may be preferred and is probably the safest generic term.

Gautama Buddha, the "founder" of Buddhism, is to be distinguished from later buddhas. *Buddha* should be capitalized in the latter instance only when used with a name.

Buddhist priests in this country usually use *the Rev.* An abbot or a Zen master may be termed *the Venerable.* The Buddhist clergy are called *priests;* most of them are monks but not all.

THE CHRISTIAN CHURCH (DISCIPLES OF CHRIST)

The Disciples is an acceptable second reference for this group, the full title of which includes the parenthetical material above.

Congregations are headed by *pastors,* and all members of the clergy are *ministers.*

CHURCHES OF CHRIST

The group calls itself a fellowship, rather than a denomination. The minister is an evangelist and is addressed as "Brother." Ministers do not use clerical titles, and their names should not be preceded by one. Do not confuse with the *United Church of Christ.*

CHURCH OF CHRIST, SCIENTIST

Christian Science Church and *Churches of Christ, Scientist* are accepted synonyms.

The church does not have clergy in the usual sense. Do not use *minister* or *pastor.* There are three principal offices: *reader, practitioner* and *lecturer.* These titles should generally be used following names and set off from them with commas. Capitalize only when used as a formal title preceding the name. Do not use on second reference. Do not use *the Rev.* in any instance.

CHURCH OF JESUS CHRIST OF LATTER-DAY SAINTS

Note the hyphen. The *d* should be lowercased in upper-lowercase spellings. The name *Mormon Church* is acceptable in all references.

The only formal titles are *president, bishop* and *elder,* which should be capitalized preceding a name. Do not use the terms *minister* and *the Rev.*

(The term *Mormon* is not properly applied to such other groups as the Reorganized Church of Jesus Christ of Latter Day Saints. Note the uppercase *d* and the lack of a hyphen.)

EASTERN ORTHODOX CHURCHES

Eastern Orthodox churches around the world include the Greek Orthodox Church, the Romanian Orthodox Church and the Russian Orthodox Church.

Some churches call their archbishop a *metropolitan;* others call him a *patriarch.* Archbishops and bishops are frequently known only by a first name. In these instances, the title should be retained on second reference: *Archbishop Iakovos; Metropolitan Nikodim.*

The honorific *Father* should be used before full names of priests, rather than *the Rev.*

EASTERN RITE CHURCHES

This group of Roman Catholic churches is not to be confused with the Eastern Orthodox.

Their archbishops are often called *patriarchs* and most commonly have only one name and retain the title on second reference.

EPISCOPAL CHURCH

This term is the generally accepted name for the Protestant Episcopal Church, the U.S. member of the Anglican Communion.

Episcopal is the adjective for an Episcopal priest. *Episcopalian* should be used only as a noun to define a church member. The adjective should be capitalized only when referring to the clergy, not when referring to bishops generically. The clergy consists of *bishops, priests* (sometimes called *ministers*), *deacons* and *brothers*. A priest who heads a parish is called a *rector* rather than a *pastor*.

For first reference to bishops: *Bishop Chester G. Kinsolving*. An alternative reference: *the Rt. Rev. Chester G. Kinsolving, bishop of Labrador*. Use the designation *the Most Rev.* only before the name of the Archbishop of Canterbury.

Do not use any of these titles on second reference.

JEHOVAH'S WITNESSES

The formal title is the Watchtower Bible and Tract Society. Members may be called *Witnesses* on second reference. They regard themselves as a society of ministers, and their churches are known as Kingdom Halls. There are no formal titles but there are four levels of ministry: *publishers, general pioneers, special pioneers* and *pioneers*.

JEWISH CONGREGATIONS

Jewish congregations are autonomous. In the United States there are three major branches of Judaism: Orthodox Judaism, Conservative Judaism and Reform Judaism. A fourth, smaller group is the Jewish Reconstructionist Foundation, whose members are called Reconstructionists.

The only formal titles are *rabbi* and *cantor*, both of which should be capitalized before a full name on first reference. Jewish congregations and the buildings that house them are generally called *synagogues*, capitalized when part of a name. Reform Jewish congregations use the word *temple* in the same way, but the generic word is *synagogue*.

LUTHERAN CHURCHES

There are three major Lutheran bodies in this country: the Lutheran Church in America, the Lutheran Church-Missouri Synod and the American Lutheran Church. In 1976, a fourth group developed when a splinter body left the Lutheran Church-Missouri Synod to form the Association of Evangelical Lutheran Churches.

The clergy are known as *ministers*. *Pastors* head congregations. In the American Lutheran Church, some officials are referred to as *bishops*. Use *Bishop* before name on first reference. Lay members are often designated as *elders, deacons* or *trustees*. Capitalize before full name on first reference. No titles on second reference.

METHODIST CHURCHES

The principal U.S. body is the United Methodist Church. Three major black denominations are: the African Methodist Episcopal Church, A.M.E. Church on second reference; the African Methodist Episcopal Zion Church, A.M.E. Zion Church; and the Christian Methodist Episcopal Church, C.M.E. Church.

The clergy are known as *bishops* and *ministers* (*pastors* when they head congregations).

PRESBYTERIAN CHURCHES

The largest U.S. body is the United Presbyterian Church (in the United States of America). Its membership is concentrated in the North, and that of the Presbyterian Church in the United States is concentrated in the South and known as the *Southern Presbyterians*.

There are four levels of authority: *congregations, presbyteries, synods* and a *general assembly* that elects a *stated clerk* and a *moderator*.

These titles should be capitalized before names on first reference.

Presbyterian ministers should be referred to on first reference as *the Rev.* No title on second reference.

QUAKERS

The full name is the Religious Society of Friends and should be used at least once in stories dealing primarily with Quaker activities. The less formal term is acceptable in all other references. The basic organizations are the weekly meeting, the monthly meeting, the quarterly meeting and the yearly meeting. References to a specific meeting should be capitalized on first reference: *the California Yearly Meeting*; on second reference, *the yearly meeting, the meeting*. Some yearly meetings form larger groups that gather less frequently: *the Friends United Meeting, the Friends General Conference*.

There is no recognized ranking of clergy above lay people. Meeting officers called *elders* or *ministers* are chosen, and some such ministers use *the Rev.* and call themselves pastors. Capitalize *elder, minister* or *pastor* before a full name on first reference. Use *the Rev.* if it is known to be the individual's preference.

ROMAN CATHOLIC CHURCH

At the top of the structure: the Pope; then cardinals, archbishops, bishops, monsignors, priests and deacons. In religious orders some men who are not ordained priests have the title *Brother*, and some women have that of *Mother* or *Sister*. Note that mothers, brothers and sisters are not part of the clergy.

Capitalize *Pope* in all instances. Other usages:

Archbishop Joseph T. McGucken of San Francisco (or *the Most Rev. Joseph T. McGucken, archbishop of San Francisco*); *Cardinal Timothy Manning; Bishop William R. Johnson of Orange* (or *the Most Rev. William R. Johnson, bishop of Orange*); *Msgr. Timothy Ferraro; Father John C. Urban* (a priest); *Deacon James L. Finnegan; Brother Walter Clark; Bother Antoninus; Sister Anne Jackson; Mother Francis Xavier Cabrini; Sister Anne.*

On second reference the last name should generally stand alone. Brothers and sisters with only one name retain the title on second reference, and sometimes colloquial usage will justify *Father John* or *Mother Mary*.

SEVENTH-DAY ADVENTIST CHURCH

Note use of hyphen, and lowercase the *d* in day. Members of the clergy are called *pastor* and *elder* and should be capitalized before full name on first reference. Do not use *the Rev.*

Use *Adventists* on second reference to the denomination.

UNITED CHURCH OF CHRIST

Many of the local groups composing it used to be the Congregational Christian Churches. Do not confuse with the *Churches of Christ.*

The clergy are *ministers* and *pastors* and are referred to on first reference as *the Rev.*

replace, supplant *Replace* suggests taking the place of a person or a thing that is destroyed, lost, worn out or otherwise gone from its position:

After Nixon gave up the presidency, he was replaced by Gerald R. Ford.

Supplant connotes a similar action involving force, fraud or innovation:

President Milton Obote of Uganda was supplanted by Idi Amin.

reportedly Most of the time there is a clearer and more graceful way around this awkward adverb, and reporters should seek it.

rerun, re-run As an unhyphenated noun this refers to a later screening of a motion picture or a TV show. As a verb, hyphenated, it refers to a physical running again of a routine, a schedule or a course.

resident See **citizen.**

restaurateur Note spelling.

restroom One word.

Resurrection Capitalize the biblical event when standing alone. But lowercase when used with the name of Jesus Christ: *a belief in the Resurrection; the resurrection of Jesus Christ.*

reverend Make it *the Rev.* before a name on first reference. On second reference, omit all honorifics. For details on which denominations use the title, see **Religious References.**

revolution Capitalize when part of a proper name: *the American Revolution, the French Revolution.* Also: *the Boxer Rebellion.* Capitalize *the Revolution* when referring to the American Revolution. Also: *the Revolutionary War.* See also **wars.**

Lowercase plurals and general references.

rial, riyal The *rial* is the basic monetary unit in Oman and Iran. The *riyal* is the basic monetary unit in North Yemen, Qatar and Saudi Arabia. See also **dinar.**

right, left For political usage, see **left.**

right field, right fielder

right-hand, right-handed, right-hander Two adjectives and a noun.

right of way

right-winger

riverbed

rock groups Do not use quotation marks on their names except in headlines when confusion is possible:

The Who, Led Zeppelin, Super Tram

roll call, roll-call Noun and adjective.

rock 'n' roll Note apostrophes. See also **R&R.**

roller skate(s), roller skater, roller-skate Two nouns and a verb.

Rolls-Royce

Roman numerals Use to designate wars or descent for people or animals: *World War II, Henry Ford II, Whirlaway II.* But never *Henry the VIII.*

Two exceptions: *SALT II, Super Bowl XIII.*

Royalty takes Roman numerals, ships don't: *Her Majesty Queen Elizabeth II, the liner Queen Elizabeth 2.*

Roman numerals are also used to designate sections of The Times.

Aircraft, missiles, satellites and space vehicles take Arabic numerals: *Pershing 4, DC-10, Apollo 8, Sputnik 1.*

Romania Not *Rumania.*

Rosh Hashanah See **High Holy Days.**

rostrum It's *on* a rostrum, *behind* or *at* a lectern, *in* a pulpit, *on* a podium.

ROTC Reserve Officers' Training Corps. Acceptable on first reference, but the term should be spelled out somewhere in the story.

rout   To *rout* is to put to flight: *They routed the enemy.* A *rout* is a headlong flight: *The battle turned into a rout.*
Not to be confused with *route.*

the Royal Family

royalty   See **Nobility and Royalty.**

rugby   Lowercase the name of the game. Capitalize the town and the school.

runaround   Noun and adjective.

run down, rundown, run-down   For example:
The engine will run down in time.
He gave me a rundown on the issue.
I am feeling run-down today; that run-down feeling.

runner-up, runners-up

runoff   Noun and adjective.

runovers   A story being run over from one page to another should break on a paragraph. But do not let it break on a colon.

rush   Do not use *rush* when the idea of speed is already implicit in the story. Use *taken* in connection with people being transported to the hospital in an ambulance; avoid *rush* in connection with police cars and fire engines.

Russ   Do not use except in headlines and then only when absolutely necessary. *Soviet* is only a little longer.

Russian Names

I. Names ending with a *-sky* (*-ski*) sound should be spelled *-sky.*
But Polish names with the same sound should be spelled *-ski.*

II. Names ending with an *-ov* or *-off* sound or with an *-ev* or *-eff* sound should be spelled *-ov* or *-ev.*
But historically or culturally familiar names should be spelled in their familiar form: *Rachmaninoff* (not *Rachmaninov*).

III. Avoid the traditional -*a* endings of women's names unless the women are prominent in their own right:

Viktoria Brezhnev (not *Brezhneva*)

But: *ballerina Maya Plisetskaya* (not *Plisetsky*)

IV. When a name begins with a *Ye-*, retain it; if it begins with an *E-*, make it *Ye-*: *Yevgeny Yevtushenko*

But do not use *y* in the interior of most names: *Dostoevsky* (not *Dostoyevsky*)

V. Spell the following names as indicated:

Alexander, Alexei, Anatoly, Andrei, Arkady, Dmitri, Fyodor, Georgy, Gorky, Grigory, Josef, Nadia, Natalia, Maxim, Pyotr, Semyon, Sergei, Tolstoy, Viktor, Viktoria, Yuli, Yuri

But spell a historically familiar name in its familiar form: *Peter the Great* (not *Pyotr*)

VI. Make it *czar*, not *tsar*.

VII. The name of the revolutionary leader is *V. I. Lenin*. The name *Nikolai* is an underground alias and should not be used.

VIII. Many Russians use two initials rather than a first name and middle initial. This is perfectly acceptable in The Times: *V. I. Lenin.*

Russians Technically speaking, the inhabitants of the Russian Soviet Socialist Republic, not those of the other republics and territories of the Soviet Union. But the word may be used casually on occasion for any resident of the Soviet Union when desired for variety.

The population and/or the government of the Soviet Union may be referred to as *Soviets*. But strive to avoid the use of *a Soviet* for an individual resident of the Soviet Union. Make it *a Soviet citizen, a Soviet official, a Soviet sailor* etc. *Soviet* is a fully acceptable adjective.

Russian may also be used to refer to residents of the old Russian Empire or former residents. But it is preferable to be more specific: *of Russian descent, of Ukrainian descent, of Uzbek descent.*

RVs Recreational vehicles. Among the more common varieties are: *motor homes* (not to be confused with *mobile homes*), *travel trailers* and *campers.*

A *motor home* is a self-propelled vehicle usually built on its own chassis, *travel trailers* are pulled by other vehicles, and *campers* are mounted on pickup trucks. See also **mobile homes.**

S

safehouse   In intelligence jargon. One word.

said, says   When an individual is quoted, directly or indirectly, the attributive verb is usually in the past tense:

> *He said, "I am tired of politics."*
> *He said he is tired of politics.*

But when a quotation, direct or indirect, is a habitual comment, the attributive verb may be in the present tense:

> *He (often) says, "I am tired of politics."*
> *He (often) says he is tired of politics.*

This use of a habitual present is sometimes overdone, and it is often preferable to avoid it or to confine it to indirect quotation. But it is permissible, and there is no compelling need to force it into the past tense to agree with other words in the same story.

There is a tendency to strain to avoid the attributive *said*, replacing it with more colorful terms. There is no need to strain. *Said* is usually the preferable word.

Do not create false attributives:

Wrong: *"Hello," he smiled.*
Wrong: *"You're out of luck," he frowned.*

Saigon   Now known as *Ho Chi Minh City*, which should be used in datelines.

saint   Abbreviate in names of holy men and in names of places: *St. Peter, St. John the Divine, St. Vibiana's Cathedral, St. Lô, St. John's (Newfoundland), St. Louis.*

In personal names, follow personal preferences.

Salonika   Not *Salonica*.

SALT Spell out on first reference to the strategic arms limitation talks. Vary abbreviation on later references with *the talks* or *the arms talks*. Acceptable in headlines. Note that it is permissible to say *SALT talks* in spite of the redundancy. Note also: *SALT II*, with Roman numerals.

saltwater

Salvadoran Not *Salvadorean* or *Salvadorian*.

samizdat The clandestine publications of dissidents in the Soviet Union. Lowercase and italicize.

San Francisco Bay Area On second reference: *the Bay Area*.

Savior Capitalize synonym for Jesus Christ.

school The compounds vary between one word and two words. For instance: *school age, school bus, school day, school year*.

But: *schoolbook, schoolchild, schoolgirl, schoolhouse, schoolmaster, schoolmate, schoolroom, schoolteacher, schoolwork, schoolyard*.

schools The correct name of the Los Angeles school district is *Los Angeles Unified School District*. It is permissible to use *Los Angeles school district* or *Los Angeles school system* except when the complete formal title is necessary.

In a similar context, it is the *Los Angeles Board of Education*, except when confusion is possible and *Los Angeles City Board of Education* may be used. Also: *Los Angeles school board, Los Angeles city school board*.

These usages vary in different communities.

For related usages, see **Capitalization** and **Academic Usages.**

science fiction Two words, no hyphen. *S-F* is acceptable in headlines in Calendar, View and Book Sections only of the Times.

Scot, Scotch, Scots, Scottish A resident of Scotland is a *Scot*. The whisky (no *e*) is *Scotch*. Otherwise, the preferred adjectives are *Scots* and *Scottish*.

Scotch tape A trade name.

Scotch whisky Others, except the Canadian, are spelled *whiskey*.

Scripture Capitalize as synonym for the Bible or its contents.

SDRs Special drawing rights. Acceptable only in financial pages.

seabed

seafood

search-and-rescue Hyphenate the adjective.

Sears, Roebuck & Co. On second reference, the company may be called *Sears*. Never *Sears & Roebuck*.

seawall

seawater

secondhand Both adjective and adverb.

secretary general Do not hyphenate. Capitalize before proper name. The plural is *secretaries general*.

secretary-treasurer Hyphenate. The plural is *secretary-treasurers*.

Secret Service

sect Avoid this word when referring to religious bodies. Many of them regard it as pejorative.

seder, seders The Jewish ritual meal.

seesaw

self- In general hyphenate: *self-defense, self-confidence, self-pity*. Some exceptions: *selfhood, selfless*.

semi- In general no hyphen: *semifinal, semiofficial*; but note: *semi-invalid*.

semicolon See **Punctuation.**

semifinal

Senate Minority Leader Capitalize. But: *Senate Republican leader, minority leader*.

senior citizen Do not use for persons under 65. See also **elderly.**

separate Note spelling.

Sequence of Tenses in Direct Quotation

I. When the main clause is in the past tense, the dependent clause is generally in the past tense as well.

President Carter said he went *to Plains to visit his mother.*
He said he would go *to Vietnam but decided against it.*
He added that his Plains trip convinced *him of the justice of his cause.*

Note that in all these instances the action or condition in the dependent clause has been in some way completed.

II. There are major exceptions to this rule, and a great deal of newspaper writing is in the realm of the exceptions.

III. The dependent clause following a verb in the past tense should be in the present tense for expressions of:

A. The habitual. *He said he* goes *to the post office every day.*
(If we said *went,* the reader would think he had stopped going.)

B. The customary. *He said there* is *always a picnic on the Fourth of July.*
(If we said *was,* the reader would think there no longer was one.)

C. The characteristic. *He said his opponent* moves *skillfully and intelligently under pressure.*
(If we said *moved,* the reader would think the opponent no longer moved in this manner.)

D. The general truth. *He said honesty* is *the best policy.*
(If we said *was,* the reader would think that this is no longer the case.)

E. The continuing. *He told me that the men* are *at work on the bridge.*
(If we said *were,* the reader would think that work had stopped.)

Note that all these exceptions, in one way or another, convey the idea of a *continuing* condition or action.

IV. The present or future tense should generally be used after a past-tense governing verb when the reference is to a point of time still felt as future at the time of writing.

He said he is going (*or* will go) *to Vietnam.*"

(If we said *was going* or *would go,* the reader would get the impression either that he had gone and returned or that he had not gone at all.)

Note that in this instance, too, one of the controlling factors is the idea of *continuing.* He *continues* to intend to go.

V. The question the writer or editor must ask himself is whether the action or condition involved is continuing:

If it is *not* continuing (i.e. has been completed), use the past.

If it *is* continuing, use the present or the future.

the Seven Deadly Sins   Anger, covetousness, envy, gluttony, lust, pride, sloth.

the Seven Dwarfs

the Seven Seas   The Arabian Sea, the Atlantic Ocean, the Bay of Bengal, the Mediterranean Sea, the Persian Gulf, the Red Sea and the South China Sea.

severe thunderstorm   When winds reach 50 m.p.h. or hail reaches three-quarters of an inch in diameter.

sewage, sewerage   *Sewage* is disposed of through a *sewerage.*

the Seychelles   These islands are an independent republic, the *Seychelles Republic. Seychelles* is plural in form but singular in construction: *The Seychelles has a seat in the United Nations.* The people of the Seychelles are referred to as *Seychellois.*

Shakespearean

Shavuot   The Jewish holiday commemorating the revelation of the law at Mt. Sinai. See also **High Holy Days.**

sheik   Note spelling. The feminine is *sheika.*

shell shock, shellshocked

Sheriff's Department In Los Angeles County. Use these capitalizations before proper names: *Sheriff's Deputy, Sheriff's Lt., Sheriff's Sgt.*

ships The names of ships do not take quotation marks. A successor ship takes an Arabic numeral: *the Queen Elizabeth 2.* Do not use the feminine pronoun. Do not use *USS* or *HMS* except in datelines. Instead use a term defining the vessel: *the U.S. aircraft carrier Nimitz.*

shoot-out The noun.

shortfall One word.

shot put, shot-putter, shot-putting

show biz A slang usage best confined to entertainment pages.

sic Avoid use as a parenthetical comment.

sic, sicked, sicking

sickout A form of protest in which employees register their disapproval by calling in sick. One word.

the Sierra Not *Sierras.*

SigAlert

sightsee, sightseer, sightseeing

sign off on Do not use this bit of government gobbledygook as a synonym for *approve* or *endorse.*

signs When signs or posters are quoted, they should be capitalized as if they were headlines:
"*This Way to the Monkey House*"
"*For Sale*"
"*Down With the Running Dogs of Capitalist Oppression*"

silk-stocking Hyphenate the adjective: *silk-stocking district.*

Sinai Desert

sit-up The noun.

the Six-Day War The Times prefers this name for the Middle East Arab-Israeli War of 1967.

sizable Not *sizeable*.

Skid Row, Skid Road Use *Skid Row* except for locations in the Pacific Northwest, where it is *Skid Road*.

skin diving The noun is two words. But hyphenate adjectives and verbs:
He skin-dived in his skin-diving equipment.

ski plane Two words.

skullcap

slam dunk Do not hyphenate when used as a noun.

slap shot

slide *Landslide* is one word. But: *earth slide, mud slide, rock slide.*

smile Not a verb of speech.
Wrong: *"How do you do," she smiled.*
Right: *"How do you do," she said, smiling.*
The same applies to such verbs as *laugh, chuckle, nod* and *grin.*

smolder Not *smoulder*.

snowpack

Socialist Capitalize the party or its members. Lowercase the philosophy or its adherents.

socioeconomic

Solid South

some Do not use as a synonym for *about*.

someday

someone

South   Capitalize to denote a specific region of the United States. Lowercase when used simply as a direction:

He grew up in the South; the fire was to the south of us.

Also: *a Southerner, the Deep South, the Solid South.*

South Boston

South-Central Los Angeles

Southern California   See **Southland.**

Southern California Association of Governments

the Southland   Southern California, not the South. For The Times' purposes, *the Southland* is conceived as that area of California that is south of a line drawn from San Luis Obispo to Fresno and then east to the state line.

Soviet, Soviets   Use to refer to the population and/or government of the Soviet Union. But try to avoid using *Soviet* as a noun for an individual. Make it *a Soviet citizen, a Soviet official, a Soviet sailor* etc. Avoid *Russ* except in headlines and then use only when necessary. See also **Russian Names.**

Soviet Bloc

space   The compounds vary: *spacecraft, spaceflight, spaceman, spaceport, spaceship, spacesuit.*

But: *space shuttle, space station, space walk.*

the Space Age

Spanish and Portuguese Names

I. Spanish and Spanish-American surnames frequently have two elements, the first the name of the father, the second that of the mother. In the case of *Gustavo Díaz Ordaz*, for instance, *Díaz* is his father's name, *Ordaz* his mother's.

But some names adhere to the older tradition of a conjunction connecting the two surnames: *José Ortega y Gasset.*

And the maternal surname is eliminated entirely in the names of many historical figures and some contemporary ones:

> *Lázaro Cárdenas, Emiliano Zapata, Luis Echeverria (Alvarez)*

On first reference The Times should use whatever is the preference of the individual, and the full name should be used if that preference cannot be ascertained:

> *Luis Echeverría* (he drops the *Alvarez*)
> *Gustavo Díaz Ordaz* (he retains the *Ordaz*)

On second reference we should abide by individual preference when it can be ascertained; when in doubt, use the doubled surname.

> *Ignacio Castro Cano; Castro* (on second reference)
> *Gustavo Díaz Ordaz; Díaz Ordaz*
> *José Ortega y Gasset; Ortega y Gasset*
> *Federico Garcia Lorca; Garcia Lorca*
> *Lázaro Cárdenas; Cárdenas*

II. In some cases the penultimate element in a name is a middle name rather than the first part of a doubled surname. In such a case repeat only the final name:

> *Carlos Rafael Rodriguez; Rodriguez*
> (*Rafael* is a middle name, *Rodriguez* a single surname.)

III. The use of doubled surnames on second reference is more prevalent in Mexico than it is elsewhere in Latin America, where the repetition of both names is being abandoned by many, depending on social status.

IV. Like the Spanish, the Portuguese frequently have doubled surnames. But, unlike the Spanish, they put the mother's name first. In the name *João Hall Themido*, *Hall* is the mother's name, *Themido* the father's.

Most Portuguese (and Brazilians) use only the father's name (the last element) on second reference, but a few use both; when in doubt use the doubled surname.

> *João Hall Themido; Themido*
> *Umberto Castello Branco; Castello Branco*

V. All these are general rules only. Many names have been altered in individual instances, either by the person involved or as a result of the varied ethnic makeup of such nations as Argentina and Brazil. The primary responsibility for correct use of these names remains that of the correspondent.

Spartan Capitalize in all instances.

Speaker Capitalize, with or without a person's name, when referring to the Speaker of a legislative body.

specialty Not *speciality*.

spell out It is redundant to say *He spelled out the details of a plan.* Make it *He spelled out a plan*, or *He gave the details of a plan.*

spinoff One word.

split infinitives The traditional taboo against splitting infinitives is largely a superstition. In many cases, if not most, the logical place for an adverb is in the middle of the infinitive construction. It is clearly better to say *to virtually complete his job* than it is to say *to complete virtually his job*, or *to complete his job virtually.*

sponsorship Name the sponsors of television programs and sports events once. Do not name them in headlines unless it is unavoidable.

sportfisherman

sport shirt

sportswriter

spot-check Hyphenate all usages.

squall A *squall* occurs when wind speeds increases suddenly by at least 16 knots, rising to 25 knots or more, and when the increase lasts at least one minute.

Sri Lanka The former Ceylon.

St. Use the abbreviation for street in numbered addresses only. For instance: *444 Wilson St., Wilson and Hendrix streets, on Hendrix Street.*

stairsteps

stakeout One word.

state To state something is to speak of it with authority or knowledge, or to express the details of. One may *state* a case, an opinion, a position or a proposition.

state colleges and universities Educational institutions in this category often have long and unwieldy names. They may often be referred to in an abbreviated form on first reference, but the full names of those that are used infrequently should appear somewhere in the story.

For instance, in California's two university systems:

UC Berkeley; University of California, Berkeley
Cal State Fullerton; California State University, Fullerton

For a full list see **Academic Usages.**

state names Abbreviate all when used with the names of cities or in datelines with the following exceptions: *Alaska, Hawaii, Iowa, Ohio, Utah.*

states Do not capitalize in such usages as *the New England states, the Western states, New York state* or *Washington state.*

But capitalize Canada's *Maritime Provinces* or *the Maritimes; the Prairie Provinces.*

Do not capitalize *state* when used to denote a state agency unless it is part of the proper name. Names of agencies should be looked up to ensure accuracy: in California, *state Board of Corrections,* but *State Board of Control.*

the States A British and Canadian reference to the United States. Also often used by Americans overseas.

stationary, stationery *Stationary* means standing still; *stationery* is writing paper.

steelmaker

stern-wheeler

stewardi Make it *stewardesses*, or better still, *flight attendants*. The word *stewardess* is not Latin, and in any case the *-i* plural in Latin is masculine.

the Stone Age

stopwatch

straights, straits When a person is in grave trouble, he is in desperate *straits*, not *straights*.

strait Almost always singular in a proper name: *Strait of Gibraltar, Juan de Fuca Strait, Strait of Taiwan, Strait of Malacca, Strait of Magellan, Dover Strait.*

An exception: *Straits of Mackinac*

straitjacket

straitlaced

the Street Synonymous with Wall Street in financial circles.

streets See **addresses and street designations.**

strip mining, strip mine No hyphens in nouns; hyphenate adjectives and verbs.

strongside, weakside One word as adjectives referring to football players: *a strongside linebacker*.

sub- As a rule no hyphen: *subatomic, subcommittee, subcompact, subdivision, sublease, submachine gun, submarine, subspecies, substation, subzero.*

subcommittees Their names should in general be lowercase, but they should be capitalized when they have acquired identities of their own:

Senate Judiciary Committee, Senate Judiciary subcommittee on court reform, Senate subcommittee on court reform, Internal Security Subcommittee

subject   See **citizen.**

subjunctive   See **were.**

Sudan   Do not use the definite article: *in Sudan*, not *in the Sudan*.

suffixes   See separate listings for: **-down, -fold, -like, -long, -off, -over, -out, -up, -wide, -wise.**
For other combinations, see Webster's New World Dictionary.
If the combination is not in the dictionary:
Use two words for the verb.
Hyphenate the noun or the adjective.

suits   A *suit* is not the same thing as a *complaint*. A *complaint* is an administrative action. A *suit* occurs when that complaint becomes a court action.

Sun Belt   Two words, just like *the Bible Belt* and *the Corn Belt.*

super-   No hyphen except for words not listed in dictionary: *supercarrier, supercharger, supermarket, supernatural, superpower, supersonic, superstar, supertanker.*
Do not use *super* as an adjective standing alone except in direct quotations.

superlatives   Beware of saying that anything is the first, most, biggest, oldest or whatever unless the superlative is positively verified. *One of the most* is almost as strong and not so open to error.

supersede   Not *supercede.*

supplant   See **replace.**

supra-   In general no hyphen: *supraliminal, supranational.*

Suriname   Not *Surinam.*

suspensive hyphenation   The audience was made up of *17- and 18-year-old girls.*

sweat pants

sweat shirt

swim, swam, swum   *Swam* is the past tense, *swum* the past participle.

He swam every day for two weeks.

He has swum every day for two weeks.

synagogue   The generic term for a Jewish house of worship is also often used as the official title by Orthodox congregations. But Reform congregations often use *Temple,* and Conservative congregations vary:

Temple Isaiah; Aatzei Chaim Orthodox Synagogue

All groups may use *Congregation* in their title:

Congregation Beth Israel

T

taboo Not *tabu*.

tailspin

tail wind

take off, takeoff Verb and noun.

take out, takeout Verb and noun or adjective.

take over, takeover Verb and noun.

tape recorder, tape-record Noun and verb.

teammate

Teamsters, Teamsters Union Capitalize references to the union or its members.

teaspoons Preferable to *teaspoonfuls*.

Tech. Sgt. Not *T. Sgt.*

teen, teen-age, teen-ager A person is in his *teens*; he is a *teen-age* athlete; he is a *teen-ager*. Do not use *teen-aged*.

Tehran Not *Teheran*.

telephone numbers When the source of a story gives the name of someone for the public to contact in connection with a program of some kind, it is clearly desirable to include instructions for such contact.
Area codes: *(123) 456-7890*

Teleprompter, TelePrompTer The first is the name of the company, the second the trade name of the product.

television *TV* is a fully acceptable synonym. *Video* should be avoided except in such compounds as *videotape*.

telex Lowercase except when part of a proper name.

temblor An acceptable synonym for earthquake. Never *tremblor*.

temple See **synagogue**.

the Ten Commandments

Texas Make it *Tex*. in datelines.

texts, transcripts Follow customary style rules for capitalization, spelling and abbreviations in handling a text or transcript.

Quotation marks should be used for material quoted in the text.

Identify a speaker with the speaker's name, in boldface, at the beginning of his speech, set off with a colon. Identify a speaker fully on first reference, follow style on second reference.

Use a similar format for question-and-answer material. See also **dialogue.**

that As a conjunction after verbs of thought or speech, the use of *that* is always permissible, but it may usually be omitted after the verb *said* when a time element does not intervene:

Carter said he had been to Europe three times.
Carter said Tuesday that he had been to Europe three times.

That should also be used when a second *that* is necessary to clarify the meaning of the sentence:

He said that he is going to Europe and that war is a possibility.

(Without the second *that*, the second clause becomes an editorial opinion.)

That should almost always be used after verbs of thought or speech other than *said*. When in doubt, use *that*.

that and **which** The pronoun *that* introduces a restrictive or defining clause that cannot be omitted from the sentence without losing its sense:

The troubles that the United States has had have been reflected in Japan.

Such clauses are never set off with commas.

The pronoun *which* introduces a non-restrictive or parenthetical clause that could be omitted:

The U.S. inflation problem, which has been serious for years, has been reflected in Japan.

Such clauses are always set off with commas.

that and **who** In general, *that* refers to persons, things or animals and *who* refers to persons only. There is nothing wrong with the use of *that* referring to persons:

the girl that I married; the girl whom I married

the The word *the* is often used when it is unnecessary and omitted when it is desirable.

It can usually be omitted before the name of a company.

It should generally be used before the names of government agencies: *the Senate, the City Council, the state Legislature.* An exception: *Congress*

Usage varies before capitalized abbreviations. In general, omit *the* before acronyms and use otherwise:

the FBI, the NAACP, the AFL-CIO, the FCC;
NASA, CORE, ASCAP, UNESCO;
Euratom, Caltrans, Amtrak, Exxon, Gemco

Do not capitalize *the* in the names of publications, except in foreign names and in second references to the Los Angeles Times: *Al Ahram, Die Welt, Le Figaro, The Times* (Los Angeles only).

See also **foreign words and phrases.**

theater, theatre Spell it *theater* except in the case of places that spell it the other way. Follow the same rule with *amphitheater.*

See also **Arts and Letters.**

theft See **burglary.**

then- Hyphenate such uses as *then-President Johnson.*

The Times Capitalize the article in second references to the Los Angeles Times.

Such a second reference is sometimes a possessive: *The Times' policy on busing.*

But when it is an adjective rather than a possessive, the article should be lowercased and the apostrophe omitted: *He is the Times correspondent in Berlin.*

Often the uses are interchangeable:

He stands by The Times' position. (Possessive)
He stands by the Times position. (Adjectival)

But the punctuation and capitalization should be consistent as indicated.

Third World

Threadneedle Street   The financial district of London.

Thrifty Drug & Discount Store   Not *Thrifty's.*

Tidewater Virginia

tiebreaker

'til   An incorrect form. Make it *till* or *until.*

time out, timeout   A person takes *time out*; an athlete asks for a *timeout.*

Times Mirror Co.   The parent company of the Los Angeles Times should be referred to as *Times Mirror Co. Times Mirror* is acceptable on second reference. Note absence of hyphen.

time zones   Use PST or PDT equivalents of times mentioned in foreign stories only when they are important, and then only in parentheses following the local time.

tip-off   Hyphenate as a noun.

titles   A person's title should usually precede his name, abbreviated: *Atty. Gen. Benjamin R. Civiletti.* Long or unwieldy titles may follow the name, set off by commas: *Drew S. Days, assistant attorney general.*

Certain titles are capitalized when they stand alone: *Pope, Dalai Lama, President.* See also **Capitalization.**

Others are capitalized when they are accompanied by a presumed or honorary jurisdiction: *Archbishop of Canterbury, Queen of England, Duke of Somerset, Kabaka of Buganda, Shah of Iran.*

But, on second reference: *the archbishop, the queen, the duke* etc.

For titles of books, paintings, films, etc., see **Arts and Letters.** See also **Nobility and Royalty.**

toe to toe, toe-to-toe   Adverb and adjective.

They squared off toe to toe; a toe-to-toe confrontation.

too   It is not necessary to set *too* off from the rest of a sentence with commas: *He is going too; this too shall pass.*

Torah   Capitalize. The first of the three major divisions of Jewish Holy Scriptures, the others being the Prophets and the Hagiographa; it is also called *the law* or the *Pentateuch. Torah* is also sometimes applied to the entire body of the Jewish Scriptures.

total, totaled, totaling

toward, backward   Do not add *s.*

town house

trade names   The trademarked names of commercial products should be capitalized and punctuated as the manufacturer does. A generic term may often be substituted. Examples appear under **Capitalization** and in the Trade Names Dictionary.

Do not rely on Webster's New World Dictionary for trade name usage.

trade winds

trampoline

trans-   Usually no hyphen: *transatlantic, transcontinental, transliteration, transpacific, transship, transsexual, trans-Siberian, transvestite.*

Corporate names present a special problem and should be checked: *Trans-World Bank, Trans World Airlines, Transcanada Pipelines, Transamerica Corp.*

Trans Alaska Pipeline System is a company that has become increasingly important in Times news stories. Since there is only one pipeline at present, the correct second reference is *the Trans Alaska pipeline* (or *the pipeline*).

But if another pipeline is considered, it would be *another trans-Alaska pipeline*.

translator   See **interpreter**.

travel, traveled, traveler, traveling

trigger   There is nothing wrong with *trigger* as a verb except for its abuse. Try using *cause, produce, signal, start* or *begin*.

Trinity   The theological concept.

trio   Use only in the musical sense. It takes singular verbs and pronouns.

TriStar   A trade name.

troop, troops, troupe   A *troop* is a group of people, usually soldiers, or animals. *Troops* means several groups but may be used simply to indicate a large number: *He called out the troops; troops surrounded the house; a thousand troops were called up.* A *troupe* is a group of entertainers. Also: *an old trouper*.

tropical depression   A cyclone with a maximum surface wind of 38 m.p.h. (33 knots).

tropical storm   A cyclone with a maximum surface wind from 39 to 73 m.p.h. (34 to 64 knots). Capitalize when part of a proper name: *Tropical Storm Teddy*.

troublemaker

trouble-shooter

Truman, Harry S.   Use a period after the initial. Some writers and editors omit the period to demonstrate their awareness that in Truman's case the letter does not stand for a name.

T-shirt

tug of war   The noun.

tune up, tuneup   The verb and the noun.

turnaround   The noun.

turnout   One word.

TV   May be used freely.

TV channels   Capitalize and spell out: *Channel 5.* Use *Ch.* in tabular matter and in schedules.

TV titles   Names of all television programs should be in quotation marks. See also **Arts and Letters.**

typhoon   See **hurricane.**

U

UCLA The abbreviation for the University of California, Los Angeles, is acceptable in The Times in all instances. The following other usages are preferred:

UCLA Hospital, UCLA School of Medicine, UCLA School of Dentistry, UCLA School of Nursing, UCLA School of Public Health, Harbor-UCLA Medical Center

UC San Francisco This branch of the University of California is also known as *UC Medical Center at San Francisco.* Either usage is acceptable.

See also **Academic Usages.**

ultra- Usually no hyphen: *ultraconservative, ultramodern, ultrasound.*

Note that *ultra* is also a noun or an adjective standing alone.

U.N. Use the abbreviation for United Nations as an adjective. Spell out the noun.

un- In general no hyphen: *unarmed, unchallenged, uncalled-for, unnamed, unnatural, unnoticed.* But: *un-American.*

under- In general no hyphen: *undercurrent, undergo, undernourished.*

undercover No hyphen: *an undercover agent.*

undersecretary The general term. But: *Under Secretary of State Lucy Wilson Benson.* The exception applies only to the U.S. government.

under way, underway One word in the nautical sense only.

UNESCO United Nations Educational and Scientific Organization.

unfeasible The preferred use is *infeasible*.

UNICEF The United Nations Children's Fund.

unified school district The correct name of the Los Angeles school district is *Los Angeles Unified School District*. It is permissible to use *Los Angeles school district* or *Los Angeles school system* except when the complete title is necessary to avoid confusion.

uninterested, disinterested See **disinterested.**

Unions

I. The full name of labor unions should generally be used: *Air Line Pilots Assn., International Chemical Workers Union, International Association of Fire Fighters, American Federation of Musicians, United Transportation Union, the Newspaper Guild.*

II. It is, however, unnecessary to use the words *of America* or similar designations in such names: *United Brotherhood of Carpenters and Joiners* (of America); *United Glass and Ceramic Workers* (of North America); *Brotherhood of Railway Carmen* (of the United States and Canada).

III. The names of a few unions are so long and unwieldy that they may be abbreviated, even on first reference, in all but the most formal of instances (such as court citations):

Make it *the Teamsters Union* rather than *the International Brotherhood of Teamsters, Chauffeurs, Warehousemen and Helpers.*

Make it *the United Auto Workers* rather than *the United Automobile, Aerospace and Agricultural Implement Workers of America.*

IV. The abbreviation *AFL-CIO* is acceptable in all uses.

V. The use of initials as abbreviations for union names should be avoided, even on second reference, unless the initials have become generally known: *ASCAP*, for American Society of Composers, Authors and Publishers; *UAW*, for United Auto Workers.

VI. The word *worker* is usually a separate word in the names of unions. An exception: *United Steelworkers.*

VII. When used generically, the word *worker* is also separate: *the auto workers, the farm workers, the steel workers.*

VIII. The words *united* and *union* usually do not occur in the same proper name. An exception: *United Transportation Union.*

IX. Note, too, that the United Firefighters of Los Angeles is a local of the International Association of Fire Fighters.

X. The word *local* should be capitalized when used with a number: *Local 219 of the Newspaper Guild, the local.*

unique   Nothing can be more or less unique.

unknown, undetermined, unidentified   It is often preferable to use *undetermined* or *unidentified* rather than *unknown:*
The future is unknown.
The fire was of undetermined origin.
The body was that of an unidentified man.

unshakable   Not *unshakeable.*

up-   Usually no hyphen: *upbeat, upstage, upstate, uptown, upturn.*

-up   Verb combinations are always two words: *to lock up, to pile up.*

Hyphenate noun combinations unlisted in Webster's New World Dictionary. Some examples of the hyphenated and the non-hyphenated:

backup, blowup, breakup, buildup, checkup, cleanup, crackup, holdup, letup, lineup, makeup, pileup, roundup, setup, smashup, stickup, sunup, tuneup, windup

call-up, cover-up, follow-up, frame-up, grown-up, mix-up, mock-up, push-up, sit-up, tie-up, shake-up, warm-up

upcoming The word *coming* is preferable.

Upper Peninsula Of Michigan.

Upstate New York

U.S., U.N. Both abbreviations should be used as adjectives. The nouns should be spelled out. Both abbreviations take periods, but it's *USIA, UNESCO* and *UNICEF.*

U.S. Army But it's *British army.* The *U.S.* may be dropped to make it *Army* unless confusion is possible.

USC Acceptable in all instances in The Times for the University of Southern California. Also: *UCLA, Caltech, County-USC Medical Center.*

U.S. News & World Report Note ampersand.

USS This abbreviation before the names of ships of the U.S. Navy should be omitted and the identification of the kind of vessel be substituted: *the U.S. aircraft carrier Nimitz.* The same applies to the British *HMS.*

But both *USS* and *HMS* should be used when appropriate in datelines.

Utah Do not abbreviate.

V

V-8 The engine and the vegetable juice.

valentine Lowercase references to a card or a gift or one's beloved:

He sent a valentine to his valentine on Valentine's Day.

The holiday is *Valentine's Day* or *St. Valentine's Day.*

value-added tax A form of indirect sales tax levied on products and services at each stage of production and distribution.

Van Dyck The painter.

Van Dyke beard, Van Dyke collar

Vegas Acceptable in headlines or for deliberate informal effect.

verbs from nouns Avoid the coinage of verbs from nouns. Some usages, like *authored* or *hosting a party,* have become common, but the good writer will avoid them. Among the undesirables: *gifted, guested, parented, paperbacked* and, worst of all, *houseguesting.*

verse Quotations of more than one line of poetry should be italicized, and each line should begin with a capital letter unless it was lowercased by the poet. But do not capitalize the first word of a line created because the poet's line was longer than the width of the column.

Each line of a passage of poetry should be indented if it is short enough to fit on a line of type. Otherwise, each line should be set flush left with a hanging indent for runover lines. Poetry should be set off from other copy by slugs without quotation marks.

When only one line, or parts of two lines, are quoted in run-in style in the middle of a sentence, italics should be omitted and quotation marks should be used. The poet's capitalization should be retained, and the end of one line should be distinguished from the beginning of the next by a virgule.

Veterans Day   No apostrophes.

vice   Do not hyphenate: *vice admiral, vice principal*. But: *viceroy*. This is an exception to Webster's New World Dictionary.

Vice President   Capitalize only when it precedes a person's name: *Vice President Walter F. Mondale, the vice president*.

videotape

Vietnam War

Virgin Mary

virgule   Use between two words to show that either is applicable (*and/or*), in dates (*3/20/79*), in fractions not available on the typewriter or computer keyboard (*4/9*) and between lines of verse as indicated under **verse**.

vitamins   Capitalize *Vitamin A, Vitamin B-12*.

volatile   Do not use as synonym for *flammable* or *explosive*.

vote of confidence   When a gesture of support for a government is offered, it is called a *vote of confidence*. But when a motion indicates lack of support for an individual, it is called a *vote of no confidence*. The British call it a *vote of censure*, but American usage prefers the former.

vs.   Use the abbreviation only in court or sports stories.

vulgarity   See **Obscenity, Profanity and Vulgarity.**

W

Wafd Not *WAFD*. An Arab political grouping.

Wailing Wall The historic wall in Jerusalem is officially known as the *Western Wall*. It may be casually referred to as the *Wailing Wall*, but not on first reference.

waist-high

wall coverings Two words.

wallposters One word when referring to the Chinese communications medium.

war horse, warhorse A *war horse* is a horse ridden in battle. A *warhorse* is a person who is a veteran of many battles, political or otherwise. The one-word form is also used for a musical or dramatic work that has become trite through overperformance.

warm up, warm-up The verb and the noun.

wars All names of wars, declared or otherwise, should be capitalized: *Boer War, Cod War, Cold War, World War II, Hundred Years' War, Six-Day War, Civil War* (in the United States), *Spanish Civil War, Vietnam War, Korean War, Yom Kippur War.*

was See **were.**

Washington state

WASP White Anglo-Saxon Protestant. May be pejorative.

water bed Two words.

weather bureau Lowercase. But: *National Weather Service.* On second reference: *weather service.*

weddings Two people are married to each other, and either one may be married to the other. Neither one marries the other.

weigh-in The noun.

weight lifter Two words.

wellspring

were, was Use the singular *were:*
—With the pronoun *you: You were foolish to do that.*
—In hypothetical first-person expressions:
   If I were you . . .
   I wish I were . . .
—In hypothetical statements with inverted word order:
   Were he my son, I would . . .
Do not use the singular *were* in a statement about the past:
He knew that if he was to win, he would have to pass.
Note that the hypothetical third-person-singular expression does not need *were:*
If he was here, I would . . .
This is a break with traditional usage but it is upheld by a number of grammarians. The late Theodore Bernstein wrote that "the subjunctive is almost a vanishing species in today's English."
Bear in mind that the greatest difficulty here is not the failure to use *were* but the misuse of it.

the West Meaning the *Western World* or the western part of the United States. Also: *the Wild West.*

West Coast Of the United States.

Western Bloc

Western(s) Capitalize when referring to movies, styles, clothing or states of mind.

Western Wall See **Wailing Wall.**

Westside, Westsiders In Los Angeles. In New York, and most other communities, it is two words: *West Side, West Sider.*

wetback   Acceptable only in quotations.

wheat field   Two words.

wheeler-dealer   Hyphenate.

where, at which   Use *where* to refer to a place *where* something occurred; use *at which* to refer to an event or an occasion *at which* something occurred:

They went together to Vietnam, where one of them was killed.
They went together to the riot, at which one of them was killed.

The same applies to *in which:*

He moved to the Detroit area, where he thrived.
He entered politics, in which he thrived.

whether   In general, either *whether* or *if* may be used to introduce a clause, and *that* may often be used as well:

I doubt whether inflation can be controlled.
I doubt if inflation can be controlled.
I doubt that inflation can be controlled.

But when the same sentence becomes negative, only *that* should be used:

I do not doubt that inflation can be controlled.

while   Use to indicate a similarity in duration of time. Avoid as a synonym for *although* or *whereas*.

whiskey, whiskeys   Use *whisky* or *whiskies* only for the Scotch or Canadian liquors.

Canadian brands vary in their spellings, some labels having *whiskey* and some *whisky*, but since Canadian spelling tends toward British rather than American conventions, *whisky* is better unless the reference is to a brand known to spell it *whiskey*.

Most Irish brands, such as Bushmill's, spell it *whiskey*.

white   See **Ethnic Designations**.

who, whom   Jacques Barzun has offered a liberalized version of the traditional rules, and The Times is adopting it.

Use *who* when the verb that follows could be placed in parentheses without damaging the sentence:

. . . *who (he believed) was one of the world's great writers.*

Use *whom* when, as direct object, you would say *him* or *her* or *them* or *us*:

Who he admired goes against the grain when the same relationship would be expressed by *he admired him* rather than *he admired he.*

But note:

. . . *who he knew was one of the country's great writers*
. . . *whom he knew to be one of the country's great writers*

If the *whom* is governed by a preposition, drop the *m* when the two words are separated by others:

Who do you wish to speak to?
To whom do you wish to speak?

Use the idiomatic *than whom.*

The real danger is not in using *who* when *whom* is correct but exactly the opposite—the misuse of *whom.*

The same general rules apply to *whoever* and *whomever.*

wide- As a rule hyphenate combinations: *wide-mouthed, wide-open, wide-ranging, wide-screen, wide-spectrum.* An exception: *widespread.*

-wide Usually one word: *citywide, countywide, nationwide, industrywide, worldwide.*

widow, wife Do not use *widow* when it is redundant: *John Smith is survived by his wife.*

Also: Do not identify an individual as a *widow* or a *widower* unless such status is relevant to the story.

windblown

winds The Beaufort scale is used officially by members of the World Meterological Organization:

Beaufort number	Miles per hour	International description
0	up to 1	Calm
1	1-3	Light air
2	4-7	Light breeze
3	8-12	Gentle breeze
4	13-18	Moderate breeze
5	19-24	Fresh breeze
6	25-31	Strong breeze
7	32-38	Moderate gale
8	39-46	Fresh gale
9	47-54	Strong gale
10	55-63	Whole gale
11	64-72	Storm
12-17	73-136	Hurricane

windswept

wine maker

Wines

I. There are several schools of thought and an entire mystique about the names of wines. The standards listed here derive from a number of authoritative sources, including The Times' own expert, Robert Balzer.

II. The names of European wines are generally derived from place names and should therefore be capitalized:

Bordeaux, Chablis, Sauternes (note the terminal *-s*), *Rioja, Burgundy, Riesling, Asti Spumante, Madeira, Marsala, Port* (from Oporto, Portugal), *Champagne, Sherry* (from Jerez, Spain), *Moselle, Rhine*

Other names of European wines are not place names and should be lowercased:

sack, vermouth, hock, claret

Also lowercased are such usages as *tête de cuvée* and *premier cru*.

III. California varietal wines and generic usages:

    A. Varietal wines are wines that are named for the variety of grape from which they are produced.

        1. The names of the GRAPES themselves are capitalized, with the modifying adjectives lowercased:

            Pinot noir, Sauvignon blanc, Zinfandel

            But: *Cabernet Sauvignon*

        2. Both elements of the names of the WINES derived from these grapes are capitalized throughout:

            Pinot Noir, Pinot Blanc, Sauvignon Blanc

    B. Generic names are generally lowercased even when they are derived from place names:

        chablis, sauterne (no terminal *-s*), *burgundy, champagne, port, sherry.*

IV. Capitalize *Cognac* and *Armagnac* and *Calvados.*

-wise Do not use hyphen in compounds meaning *in the direction of* or *in regard to: clockwise, jobwise, otherwise.*

But make it *penny-wise* and *street-wise* because here the compound has a different meaning.

Do not coin *-wise* words.

witch hunt, witch hunting, witch hunter Three nouns. But hyphenate the adjectival usage: *He embarked on a witch-hunting campaign.*

women's liberation movement, women's lib Lowercase both usages. Use *women's lib* only in direct quotations or for deliberate informal effect.

women's wear

wondrous Not *wonderous.*

work There is no rule for the formation of compounds. Some examples: *work basket, work camp, work farm, work force, work sheet;*

workbench, workbook, workday, workhorse, workhouse, work-load, workman, workout, workplace, workshop, worktable, work-week.

-workers Generally two words: *iron workers, textile workers.* An exception: *woodworkers.* See also **Unions.**

workout One word.

world-famous

worship, worshiped, worshiper

write off, write-off Hyphenate the noun and the adjective.

write in, write-in Hyphenate the noun and the adjective.

writ of certiorari Italicize the entire phrase. It means that a higher court has called up the record of a lower court for review. It is preferable to say that the higher court has agreed to review the case.

writ of mandamus Italicize the entire phrase. It is simply a court order and is best described that way.

X

x In lumber measurements: a 2x4.

x, x'd, x'ing As a verb.

Xerox Capitalize in all instances.

Xinhua The New China News Agency. Use translation in all
instances.

Xmas Do not use.

X-rated

X-ray Capitalize and hyphenate all usages.

Y

yak, yakked, yakking   Also *yak-yak* and *yakety-yak*.

year-end   Hyphenate both noun and adjective.

Yemen, South Yemen   Use *Yemen* for the Yemen Arab Republic, the capital of which is Sana and which lies along the Red Sea. Use *South Yemen* for the People's Democratic Republic of Yemen, the capital of which is Aden and which lies along the Gulf of Aden and the Arabian Sea.

yoga, yogi   *Yoga* is the discipline, a *yogi* its practitioner.

yogurt

Yom Kippur War

yoo-hoo

Young Turks

youngster   Apply only to children except in direct quotations.

youth   The word may be used as a collective for young people as a whole or to designate a boy between the ages of 13 and 18. Persons above 18 are men or women.

yo-yo   No longer a trade name. Lowercase.

yule, yuletide   Lowercase.

Z

ZANU, ZAPU The Zimbabwe African National Union and the Zimbabwe African People's Union. On first reference each should be spelled out in full. On second reference the acronyms are permissible, but it is preferable to say *the people's union* or *the national union* when the reference is clear. The acronyms may be used in headlines if necessary. Together the two groups constitute the Patriotic Front.

Zen

zero-zero Weather conditions when both ceiling and visibility are zero.

zigzag

zilch Lowercase the slang expression for zero or nothing.

ZIP code Thus: *San Francisco, Calif. 92304.*

zip gun

Zzyzx You may not believe it, but it's a good one to end an alphabetical listing with. This community near Baker was founded as a religious and health spa and is now being used as a base for desert studies by a consortium of seven California colleges. It was named with the intention of its being "the last word in the language," and it surely is.

Bibliography

Few of these works have been cited directly in this book, but all have had an influence in its preparation.

Angione, Howard (ed.). *The Associated Press Stylebook and Libel Manual*. The Associated Press. New York. 1977.

Barzun, Jacques. *Simple & Direct: A Rhetoric for Writers*. Harper & Row. New York. 1975.

Bernstein, Theodore M. *The Careful Writer: A Modern Guide to English Usage*. Atheneum. New York. 1977.

Bernstein, Theodore M. *Dos, Don'ts and Maybes of English Usage*. New York Times Books. New York. 1977.

Congressional Quarterly and Editorial Research Reports Stylebook. Congressional Quarterly. Washington, D.C. 1976.

Copperud, Roy H. *American Usage and Style*. Van Nostrand Reinhold. New York. 1979.

Curme, George O. *English Grammar*. Barnes & Noble. New York. 1961.

Evans, Bergen and Cornelia. *A Dictionary of Contemporary English Usage*. Random House. New York. 1957.

Flesch, Rudolf, and Lass, A. H. *A New Guide to Better Writing*. Harper & Row. New York. 1949.

Follett, Wilson. *Modern American Usage*. Hill & Wang. New York. 1966.

Fowler, H. W. *A Dictionary of Modern English Usage*. Oxford University Press. New York. 1965.

Gowers, Sir Ernest. *The Complete Plain Words*. Penguin Books. Baltimore, Md. 1963.

Jordan, Lewis (ed.). *The New York Times Manual of Style and Usage*. New York Times Books. New York. 1976.

Shaw, Harry. *Dictionary of Problem Words and Expressions*. McGraw-Hill. New York. 1975.

U.S. News & World Report Stylebook for Writers and Editors. U.S. News & World Report Inc. Washington, D.C. 1977.

Webb, Robert A. *The Washington Post Handbook on Style*. McGraw-Hill. New York. 1978.

Among the outside consultants who have made significant contributions to this book are:

Hamid Algar and Amin Sweeney of the University of California at Berkeley; Waleed Alkhateeb, DeWayne B. Johnson, Charles Kaplan and Kambiz Maani of California State University, Northridge; Seeger Bonebakker, Ismail Poonawala, Mehri Reid and Damodar SarDesai of UCLA; Edwina Iredale of the British Consulate General in Los Angeles; Donald Clay Johnson of the University of Wisconsin, and Eileen Alt Powell of the Associated Press.

MERIDIAN Books You'll Enjoy

☐ **THE SELECTED POETRY OF POPE edited and with an Introduction by Martin Price.** Presented here in their entirety are several of Pope's principal works, including *Windsor Forest, Essay on Man, Essay on Criticism* and his masterpiece, *The Dunciad.*
(#F532—$4.95)

☐ **THE SELECTED POETRY AND PROSE OF WORDSWORTH edited and with an Introduction by F. Hartman.** This volume includes Wordsworth's immortal lyrics, ballads, sonnets, and autobiographical poems, as well as a generous selection of his prose —including his *Preface to Lyrical Ballads,* one of the landmark critical statements in our literature. (#F533—$5.95)

☐ **THE SELECTED POETRY OF DONNE edited and with an Introduction by Marius Bewley.** This collection of Donne's first poetry includes the complete *Songs and Sonnets, Elegies, Epithalamions, Satyres,* and *Letters to Several Personages:* "The Storm", "To the Countess of Bedford", "To the Countess of Huntingdon"; plus *The Second Anniversary, The Progress of the Soul,* and selections from *Divine Poems.* (#F517—$4.95)

☐ **JONATHAN EDWARDS: Basic Writings selected, edited, and with a Foreword by Ola Elizabeth Winslow.** These selections extend from Edwards' first essays as a youthful prodigy to the great sermons and treatises of his maturity; they offer both a fascinating record of spiritual evolution and a body of intellectual achievement of truly enduring import. (#F489—$4.95)

In Canada, please add $1.00 to the price of each book.

Buy them at your local bookstore or use this convenient coupon for ordering.

THE NEW AMERICAN LIBRARY, INC.
P.O. Box 999, Bergenfield, New Jersey 07621

Please send me the PLUME and MERIDIAN BOOKS I have checked above. I am enclosing $_____(please add $1.50 to this order to cover postage and handling). Send check or money order —no cash or C.O.D.'s. Prices and numbers are subject to change without notice.

Name_____

Address_____

City_____State_____Zip Code_____

Allow 4-6 weeks for delivery.
This offer is subject to withdrawal without notice.

The MERIDIAN Quality Paperback Collection

☐ **THE NOBILITY OF FAILURE: Tragic Heroes in the History of Japan by Ivan Morris.** This brilliantly detailed and sympathetic work portrays the lives of nine heroes from Japanese history, beginning with a legendary fourth-century prince and concluding with the kamikaze fighters of World War II. "A panoramic sweep across 1500 years . . . fascinating . . . beautifully recounted . . . elegantly written."—*New Republic*
(#F522—$5.95)

☐ **THE NEW ARCHAEOLOGY by David Wilson.** A brilliant survey of the revolutionary scientific techniques that are expanding our knowledge of the past. "Full, lucid, and interesting."—*Washington Post* (#F448—$5.95)

☐ **THE CRIME SOCIETY: Organized Crime and Corruption in America edited by Francis A. J. Ianni and Elizabeth Reusslanni.** This volume presents the most notable work of leading scholars, crime experts, and government commissions in learning the truth about organized crime in America, offering an unrivaled overview of organized crime as both a historical and vital segment of the American economy. (#F450—$5.95)

☐ **ADVICE AND DISSENT: Scientists in the Political Arena by Joel Primack and Frank Von Hippel.** The dangers of mixing technology and politics behind closed doors—and how a new breed of scientists is taking the issues to the public. "Recommended reading for everyone."—*Library Journal* (#F443—$3.95)

☐ **COCAINE PAPERS by Sigmund Freud. Notes by Anna Freud. Edited and with an Introduction by Robert Byck, M.D.** This book traces the history of cocaine in the nineteenth century, including a wealth of previously unpublished and unavailable writing both by and about Freud. Personal letters and the early dream analyses reveal Freud's significant course from experimentation with cocaine to the writing of his masterpiece—*The Interpretation of Dreams.* (#F431—$4.95)

☐ **THE WRITINGS OF MARTIN BUBER edited by Will Herberg.** Buber's original views on existence, society, faith, Jewish destiny, teaching, and learning. Fascinating insights into the Hasidic and Zionist movements, as well as the writings of those who influenced him. (#F538—$4.95)

Buy them at your local bookstore or use coupon on
next page for ordering.

℗